SHARKS

Michael Bright

FIREFLY BOOKS

A Firefly Book

Published by Firefly Books Ltd. 2011

First printing

Publisher Cataloging-in-Publication Data (U.S.)
Bright, Michael
     Sharks / Michael Bright.
[128] p. : ill., col. photos. ; cm.
Includes bibliographical references and index.
Summary: Describes the broad range of sharks living throughout the world, their biology and behavior.
ISBN-13: 978-1-55407-988-9 (pbk.) 1. Sharks. I. Title.
597.3 dc22   QL638.9.B738 2011

Library and Archives Canada Cataloguing in Publication
A CIP record of this book is available from Library and Archives Canada (CDN)

Published in the United States by
Firefly Books (U.S.) Inc.
P.O. Box 1338, Ellicott Station
Buffalo, New York 14205

Published in Canada by
Firefly Books Ltd.
66 Leek Crescent
Richmond Hill, Ontario L4B 1H1

Printed in China by C&C Offset

Developed by:
Natural History Museum
Cromwell Road
London SW7 5BD

Designed by Mercer Design, London
Reproduction by Saxon Digital Services
Printed by C&C Offset, China

Front cover: © Reinhard Dirscherl/Photolibrary
Back Cover: © Howard Hall/Seapics.com

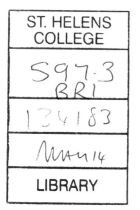

Contents

CHAPTER 1
Shark biology and behaviour

THERE ARE OVER 460 KNOWN species of sharks, ranging in size from the gigantic whale shark to the miniature dwarf shark, and they come in all manner of shapes, each adapted to its own peculiar niche in the sea. There are, for instance, flat-packed anglesharks that hug the seabed, torpedo-bodied blue sharks that wander the open ocean, weird-looking goblin sharks with long, dagger-like snouts that dwell in the deep sea, eel-shaped frilled sharks, wobbegongs that resemble seaweed-encrusted rocks, highly-manoeuvrable hammerheads with bizarre-shaped heads, megamouths with cavernous mouths and thick lips, deep-sea sharks that glow in the dark and thresher sharks with amazingly long, scythe-shaped tails.

OPPOSITE When hunting fur seals off the South African coast, a great white shark accelerates so rapidly – at least 40 km/h (25 mph) and maybe up to 56 km/h (35 mph) – that it fails to stop on reaching the surface and shoots out of the water. The spectacle is all over in as little as two seconds.

JAWS AND TEETH

The 'business' end of the shark is its head, with powerful jaws and row upon row of formidable teeth. The mouth of most hunting sharks is on the underside of the head and can be thrust forward when biting prey. Aristotle, the famous Greek naturalist and philosopher of the 4th century BC, thought otherwise. He suggested that sharks had to turn on their sides when they attack, and this was perpetuated for centuries. Now, we know this is not true. In a research programme in the early 1960s led by Perry Gilbert at the Lerner Marine Laboratory, on the island of Bimini in the Bahamas, the lemon shark, *Negaprion brevirostris*, was videoed and the results analysed. This shark is an active hunter capable of rapid acceleration. When approaching its target at speed, it brakes with its pectoral fins, raises its snout, drops its lower jaw, protrudes its upper jaw and teeth, and then jabs forwards several times to get a good grip. It then rips and tears the flesh of its victim by shaking its head from side to side. More recent work by Cheryl Wilga and Philip Motta, University of South Florida, USA with brownbanded bamboosharks, *Chiloscyllium punctatum*, revealed that at the moment the shark bites, the protruding upper jaw retracts under the head, pulling the prey into the mouth. The strength of a shark's bite, however, is less than one might imagine. In tests, sharks show an average tooth-tip pressure of 49,167 kg/cm^2 (42,674 lb/in^2) on a 2 mm (0.08 in) square tip, compared to a human measurement of 34,564 kg/cm^2

TOP The partly open mouth of this sand tiger shark, *Carcharias taurus*, seems to be overflowing with sharp, pointed teeth that it uses to grasp slippery squid and fish.

MIDDLE The tiger shark, *Galeocerdo cuvier*, possesses rows of teeth that resemble the blades of a chain saw, which it uses to slice through flesh, sinew and bone.

BOTTOM The rows of tiny, needle-sharp teeth in the large mouth of the swell shark, *Cephaloscyllium ventriosum*, are used to grab bottom-living fishes and crustaceans.

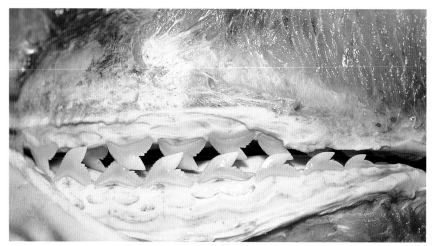

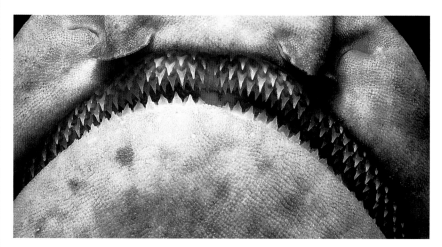

(30,000 lb/in^2). The difference is that humans have few, relatively blunt teeth, whereas many species of sharks have several rows of extremely sharp, razor-shaped or pin-shaped teeth, capable of inflicting considerable damage (see great white shark, p.52).

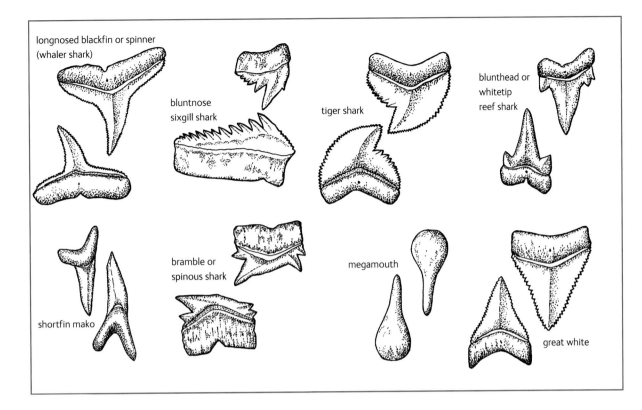

longnosed blackfin or spinner
(whaler shark)

bluntnose
sixgill shark

tiger shark

blunthead or
whitetip
reef shark

bramble or
spinous shark

megamouth

shortfin mako

great white

Tooth shape varies with diet. The shortfin mako shark, *Isurus oxyrinchus*, and the sand tiger shark, *Carcharias taurus*, have sharp, pointed teeth with which they grab slippery fish and squid. The tiger shark, *Galeocerdo cuvier*, has serrated teeth, resembling those in a chainsaw. It can slice through flesh and bone, and even the tough carapaces of sea turtles. The horn shark, *Heterodontus francisci*, has two types of teeth – small, sharp ones at the front of the mouth for catching small fish, and flat, pavement-like teeth at the back for crushing the tests, or shells, of sea urchins. The tooth shape of the great white shark, *Carcharodon carcharias*, changes with age. When young, this formidable predator has pointed teeth for grabbing fish, but on maturing, it develops triangular, saw-like teeth in the upper jaw for carving through the flesh of sea mammals, and awl-like, grasping teeth in the lower jaw for holding its prey steady – rather like the knife-and-fork combination.

Shark's teeth drop out a great rate. The lemon shark loses a row every eight days, and the loss can be seasonal. The nurse shark, *Ginglymostoma cirratum*, drops one row every ten days in summer when the feeding is good, but in winter loses only one row in two months because it feeds less often. This is far from being a problem for the sharks; it is part of a wonderfully efficient system of tooth replacement for a creature that depends so much on them. The teeth are borne on a 'conveyor belt' arrangement, with newly developing teeth at the back and the full-grown teeth at the front. The new ones move forward when the old ones are damaged, blunted or drop out, and in this way are replaced endlessly throughout life.

ABOVE Sharks can be identified from their teeth alone. Each species has teeth of a distinct size and shape depending on its eating habits, and some species have differently-shaped teeth at various stages of their development.

DIGESTIVE SYSTEM

This emphasis on efficient feeding is reflected also in the shark's digestive system. On average, a shark must eat between 0.6 and 3% of its body weight each day in order to survive. Sluggish sharks, such as the nurse shark, are at the lower end of the scale, while the extremely active shortfin mako shark requires a whole lot more food. A 64 kg (140 lb) mako needs to eat about 1.8 kg (4 lb) of fish each day just to stay alive, and it must increase this daily requirement to more than 2.5 kg (5½ lb) to compensate for any high-speed chases.

In order to help this process, the shark has an expandable stomach capable of receiving large quantities of food in one sitting. This is important for any species that scours the open ocean, such as the oceanic whitetip shark, *Carcharhinus longimanus*, whose food is widely scattered and whose next meal is far from certain. Some species, such as the great white and mako, ensure food is dealt with quickly by having a body that is warmer than the surrounding seawater and a warm stomach. A mako therefore, is able to digest a meal within one or two days, whereas other hunters, such as the sandbar shark, *Carcharhinus plumbeus*, and blue shark, *Prionace glauca*, take an average of three days to digest a similar quantity of food.

All sharks have a relatively short gut, which is equipped internally with a special valve structure. Some species, such as thresher, great white and mako sharks, have a spiral-shaped valve, like a spiral staircase, while others, such as sandbar, dusky and tiger sharks, have a scroll-shaped valve that can be unravelled in a dead specimen to reveal a single sheet of mucous tissue. Each species has a valve of a different design, and some closely related species, such as deep-sea lantern sharks, *Etmopterus* spp., are difficult to tell apart except for the number of twists and turns in their spiral valves. The valve arrangement slows down the passage of food, allowing digestion to take place more effectively and nutrients to be absorbed more efficiently. But there is a downside too, to this arrangement.

RIGHT This bronze whaler or copper shark, *Carcharhinus brachyurus*, has been killed in Australian waters. It has everted its stomach through its mouth during the struggle – a response that often occurs spontaneously when a shark is caught or placed in an aquarium.

PARASITES AND DISEASE

With slow food throughput, the intestinal valve is a favourite lodging site for internal parasites, most notably tapeworms. They spend all of their lives not just in one species of shark but only in a single section of its valve. The dusky smoothhound or smooth dogfish, *Mustelus canis*, for example, has a spiral valve with eight chambers. The first three are occupied by tapeworms with the tongue-twisting scientific names *Protochristianella*, *Lacistorhynchus* and *Calliobothrium lintoni*, while the fourth is home to *Calliobothrium verticillatum*. By the time food has reached the fifth chamber, much of the nutrients have been removed, so the rest of the chambers are unoccupied. Parasites are a fact of life for sharks. There are parasitic copepods that saunter in and out of their gills and nasal passages or attach themselves firmly to the edges of their fins, and marine leeches that make a nuisance of themselves around the cloacal area, but surprisingly, sharks are usually untroubled by serious natural diseases. Contrary to popular belief, sharks do get cancers but they are relatively rare. The Smithsonian Institution's *Registry of Tumours in Lower Animals* lists many tumours in bony fishes, but few in sharks and rays.

Sharks were most probably among the first creatures to have developed an effective immune system, and during the past several hundred million years their bodies have evolved all manner of defence systems against disease. They have high levels of an immuno-globulin circulating in the blood, for instance, that is ready to destroy or disable virtually any invading organism at any time. Immune cells are produced in the spleen, thymus, gonads and oesophagus, rather than just in the bone marrow as with mammals. They circulate in the blood, ready to go to work with hardly any lag between infection and response. As a result, sharks can live long and relatively healthy lives if left unmolested, but they are slow to grow and mature. Tagging studies in the northwest Atlantic have shown that the sandbar shark, for example, may live for 40 to 50 years but does not reach sexual maturity until it is 30 years old.

LEFT External parasites live on a whitetip reef shark, *Triaenodon obesus*, but many are removed by tiny, striped cleaner fish that slither all over the shark's head, including inside its gills and mouth.

HITCH-HIKERS

Small fish frequently accompany sharks. Some crowd around sharks for protection. Off Cape Hatteras, on the US east coast, large sand tiger sharks are seen surrounded by clouds of 'bait fish' (fish of any species less than about 15 cm/6 in long). Here the latter are safer from the predatory attentions of passing amberjacks, *Seriola dumerili*, and barracuda, *Sphyraena* spp. Other shark species, especially oceanic whitetip sharks, have small black-and-white striped pilot fish, *Naucrates doctor*, that swim just ahead of their snout. Once it was believed they guided the shark, hence their common name, but now it is thought that because sharks tend to be messy eaters they simply take advantage of the scraps of food scattered in the water. Close to a shark's head is a relatively safe place to be.

The whale shark, *Rhincodon typus*, often has yellow-and-black striped pilot fish swimming ahead of its enormously wide, slit-like mouth. They are the young of golden trevally, *Gnathanodon speciosus*, a fish more usually found in large shoals close to coral reefs. They stay with the shark until mature, then take their leave and join a large school where there is safety in numbers. They lose their body stripes but retain yellow fin tips.

Among the most conspicuous hitchhikers are remoras or sharksuckers, *Remora remora, Echeneis naucrates and Remorina albescens*. Like a living adornment, a remora has a special adaptation of its dorsal fin that enables it to ride on the shark's underside. The dorsal fin is modified into a sucker-like structure on the top of the remora's head. The flattened fin rays resemble a rubber or crepe sole of a shoe, and are used to create a vacuum between the remora and the shark. With this device the remora can cling tightly and travel the ocean for free, no matter how fast its host might go. Remoras feast on their host's other hangers-on, the parasitic copepods and isopods, or fish lice, and clean up the scraps from their meal. In the Bahamas, remoras accompanying female lemon sharks dart out and consume afterbirth debris directly after the pups are born.

Remoras have their own hitchhikers, in particular, parasitic flatworms that live on their gills. The larval flatworm lives on the skin of the remora's shark companion and uses it to switch hosts. The flatworm lays eggs on the remora's gills. The eggs hatch and the larvae transfer to the shark's skin. When the remora changes sharks, the larvae are ready to move to their new host, where they develop into adult flatworms.

ABOVE A gigantic whale shark, *Rhincodon typus*, with a group of young golden trevally, *Gnathanodon speciosus*, swimming ahead of its snout and remoras attached to the underside of its head.

BELOW LEFT These 'bait' fish gain safety from predation by crowding around a sand tiger shark, *Carcharias taurus*.

BELOW RIGHT A remora swims below its temporary host, a Caribbean reef shark, *Carcharhinus perezi*.

GROWTH CHANGES

Growth rates vary from species to species. Similar tagging returns have revealed that the shortfin mako grows up to 50 cm (20 in) during its first year and 30 cm (12 in) each year thereafter. The sand tiger shark in the Atlantic grows about 25–30 cm (10–12 in) in year one, but each year thereafter its growth rate declines by 5 cm (2 in) every two years until it reaches a minimum rate of 5–10 cm (2–4 in) per year. Bull sharks, *Carcharhinus leucas*, tagged in the Gulf of Mexico grow 15–20 cm (6–8 in) a year during their first five years, 10 cm (4 in) a year for years six to ten, 5–7 cm (2–2.8 in) in years eleven to sixteen, and less than 4–5 cm (1.6–2 in) each year thereafter. All of these sharks are thought to live to 25 or more years.

Some species change shape and colour as they grow. Young makos have short, rounded dorsal fins, which become tall, triangular and sharp-pointed when they mature. Newborn tiger sharks have leopard-like blotches, but these join to form tiger-like stripes, and then fade altogether when older. Males and female sharks tend to grow at the same rate at first, but later the females outstrip the males so that mature female sharks tend to be larger.

BREATHING

Whatever their size, like any animal, all sharks must breathe. It is sometimes said that sharks must keep moving in order to breathe or sink to the bottom and drown, but this is only partly true. Some sharks, such as the whitetip reef shark and nurse shark and especially, bottom-dwelling species such as carpetsharks, wobbegongs and angelsharks, are able to rest on the sea floor and pump water over their gills, where they extract the oxygen it contains. They open their mouth, expand the walls of the pharynx, and cause the water to rush in. By closing the mouth and raising the floor, the water is propelled over the gills and out through the gill slits. Other species, such as the oceanic whitetip shark and grey reef shark, really do have to keep moving or they are in trouble. They adopt a system known as obligate ram ventilation in which oxygen-rich seawater passes freely through the open mouth and pharynx, over the gills and out through the gill slits as they swim forwards. Most modern sharks possess five pairs of gill slits, but more primitive species, such as the appropriately-named sixgill and sevengill sharks, have more.

BELOW This whitetip reef shark can rest on the floor of its coral reef home because it is able to pump water through its mouth and over its gills, without having to swim forwards.

SWIMMING

Sharks swim by passing a series of waves down the body. First the head oscillates from side to side, and then the amplitude of the movement becomes progressively greater towards the tail. This pushes a series of inclined surfaces outwards and backwards against the water which, when pushed aside, causes the shark to move forwards. The tail shape varies with lifestyle. Fast-swimming sharks, such as the makos and great white, have tail fins with an almost equal upper and lower lobe, a feature they share with other fast swimmers, such as swordfish and sailfish. Others, such as the tiger shark, have a tail with a longer upper lobe, its function a subject of debate amongst shark scientists. Some think that it creates a thrust that is directed ventrally through the shark's centre of gravity, while others believe that it produces a downward thrust that is countered by the shark's pectoral fins.

The pectoral fins are like an aircraft's wings, and together with the pelvic fins, they provide the upward force of lift when the shark moves forwards. In cross-section, they have the leading edge slightly thicker than the trailing edge, and as water passes above and below the fin it moves more quickly over the top than the bottom surface. A partial vacuum forms on the upper side and a slight pressure pushes up on the underside that is sufficient to pull the fin, and the shark attached to it, upwards. Experiments conducted by Cheryl Wilga while at the University of Rhode Island, USA, using lasers and clouds of tiny silver-covered glass balls in a similar way to the use of smoke in wind tunnel experiments, have revealed that the shark's body itself is also an important surface for providing lift. The most charismatic external body part however, must be the dorsal fin, often seen cutting through the surface of the sea

BELOW The shape of a shark's tail depends on its function. High-speed sprinters have equal upper and lower lobes; open ocean hunters have tails with slightly larger upper lobes for cruising; and slow-swimming bottom-dwellers have large flat tails or tails with very large upper lobes. The extraordinarily long upper lobe of a thresher shark's tail is an adaptation for stunning prey.

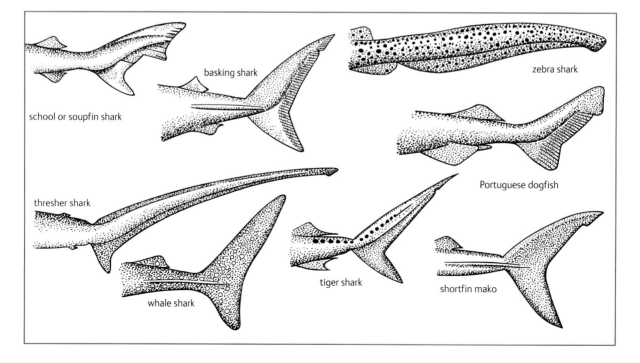

school or soupfin shark

basking shark

zebra shark

thresher shark

Portuguese dogfish

whale shark

tiger shark

shortfin mako

SHARK SKIN

Sharks are highly efficient swimmers. The streamlined shortfin mako has been seen to leave the water at speeds estimated to be in excess of 75 km/h (46 mph). It achieves this remarkable feat partly with a hydrodynamic body shape and powerful swimming muscles, but also with the help of its skin. Shark skin is covered with tiny 'teeth', or dermal denticles, and each species has denticles of a different shape. They are the shark's secret weapon. You can feel the denticles if you stroke a shark. If you move your hand from front to back it appears to be smooth, but if you brush the opposite way the skin feels like a carpenter's rasp. This is because, on most sharks, the flattened crown of each denticle points towards the tail. One of the exceptions is the slow-swimming basking shark. Its skin feels rough whichever way you stroke it. These more sluggish sharks also have larger denticles, whereas the streamlined speed merchants have tightly packed smaller denticles, which offers a clue to their main function. Aside from providing the shark with a 'chain-mail suit' for protection, they are important in shark hydrodynamics. These 'skin teeth' protrude from the skin and are aligned in such a way that they channel the water across the shark's body in the most efficient way. They also work in the interface between skin and water, reducing drag by as much as 8% and allowing the shark to slide through the sea. In experiments during the 1980s at Scripps Institution of Oceanography, California, the efficiency of a blue shark was compared to that of a submarine and, weight for weight, the shark required six times less driving power. This discovery has led designers of racing yachts, submarines, aircraft and even bathing suits to experiment with rough rather than smooth surfaces for their products. The results in terms of energy saving have been remarkable. The skin teeth also confer sharks with a predatory advantage: stealth. Bony fish are generally noisy swimmers, but sharks are silent hunters. They can sidle right up to their prey and it would not even have heard them coming.

BELOW A shark's skin is covered by tiny tooth-like dermal denticles or 'skin teeth'. Surprisingly, the shark's rough skin is hydrodynamically more efficient than shiny, smooth skin.

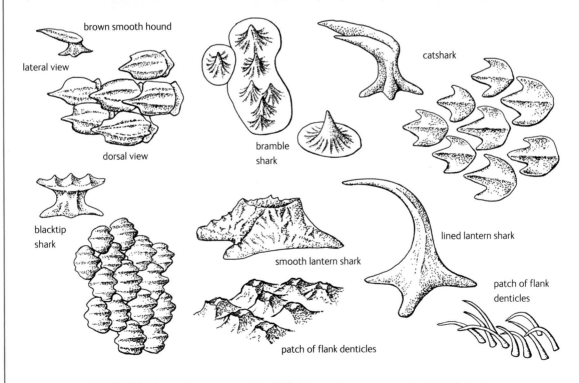

brown smooth hound

lateral view

dorsal view

bramble shark

catshark

blacktip shark

smooth lantern shark

lined lantern shark

patch of flank denticles

patch of flank denticles

in scary shark films. Many sharks have two – a larger anterior and smaller posterior dorsal fin – and these help keep the shark upright, preventing it from rolling. They also assist in making tight turns.

Forward motion, the shark's body and its wing-like pectoral fins may help keep a shark up, but this is aided by its main buoyancy aid, an oil-filled liver. Some bottom-dwelling sharks, such as dogfish sharks, have livers that are 90% oil. The oil is less dense than water, indeed it floats at its surface, so the unusually large liver in most sharks helps keep them afloat. The basking shark, *Cetorhinus maximus*, which can grow to over 9 m (30 ft) long, has a gigantic twin-lobed liver that is a quarter of its body weight and runs the entire length of its abdominal cavity.

In one shark species, the sand tiger shark, the upper 60% of its stomach has a thinner lining with far less cells secreting digestive juices than the lower part. This enables the sand tiger to store gulps of air in the upper part, so that it can hover almost motionless in the water, the only shark known to do so.

SHARK INTELLIGENCE

Sharks are not noted for their intelligence, but they are smarter than one might think. With a high brain size to body weight ratio, some sharks have the capacity to carry out 'intelligent' tasks. In captivity, lemon sharks, *Negaprion brevirostris*, and nurse sharks, *Ginglymostoma cirratum*, have been taught to discriminate coloured discs and different shapes, ring bells in response to offers of food, negotiate mazes and recover rings like dolphins. In 1975, for example, Samuel Gruber at the University of Miami's Rosenstiel School of Marine and Atmospheric Science, discovered that lemon sharks learn classic conditioning tasks up to 80 times faster than cats or rabbits, and that they are able to remember visual discrimination tests for up to a year without retraining. They also show spatial preferences, akin to 'handedness' in mammals. In the wild, shortfin mako sharks, *Isurus oxyrinchus*, have rapidly learned to distinguish between a black circle shape that rewards them with a juicy fish and a black square shape that offers them an inedible model fish. The tests also show that mako sharks use sight as their main sense when approaching close to their target, but like most other sharks, employ an entire battery of senses to locate it.

A BATTERY OF SENSES

A shark is like a modern warship, an integrated weapons system, with an extraordinary array of sensors, probably the most diverse of any known predator. Low-frequency sounds tend to travel great distances underwater, so a shark's auditory system could be the first sense to pick up an interesting target. A part of the inner ear, known as the macula neglecta, responds to vibrations coming through the top of the skull, giving hunting sharks the ability to pick up underwater sounds coming from the front and above. Rapid, irregularly-pulsed, broad-band sounds at frequencies below 600 hertz, similar to those made by injured prey or a group of spawning fish, can alert

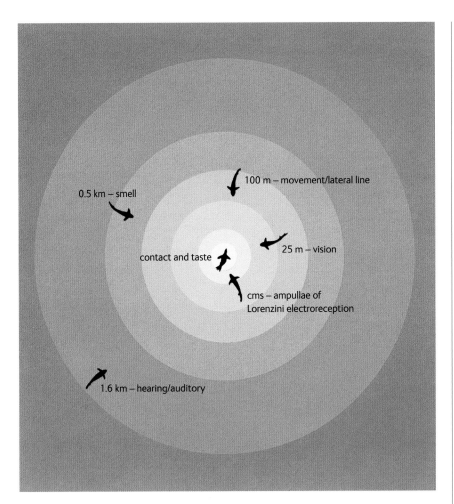

0.5 km – smell

100 m – movement/lateral line

contact and taste

25 m – vision

cms – ampullae of
Lorenzini electroreception

1.6 km – hearing/auditory

LEFT Each of the shark's many senses are sensitive to stimuli from prey at different ranges.

a hunter such as a bull shark, *Carcharhinus leucas*, from over 1.6 km (1 mile) away. At a distance of 0.5 km (1/3 mile), it is able to smell blood in the water and follow a trail back to the source. It can detect one part of fish extract in 25 million parts of seawater, the equivalent of ten drops of blood in an average-sized municipal swimming pool. The odour in the water is swept into a pair of nasal openings, one on each side of the snout, by the forward motion of the shark. Inside are some convoluted plumping and folded plates of odour-sensitive cells. At the University of Bath, Jonathan Cox is investigating the flow of water through a hammerhead shark's nose using a preserved specimen from the Natural History Museum in London. Computerised tomography (CT) scans reveal that there is a main U-shaped channel and many smaller channels leading from it, and the sensory cells are in the smaller channels.

The shark is able to locate the odour source by comparing the time odour molecules hit each nostril, turning towards whichever side picks up the scent first. It had been long thought that sharks compare the concentration of the odour, but at the University of South Florida, Jayne Gardiner, together with research teams from other marine laboratories in the USA, found that the physics is flawed. Fluids disperse chaotically, with peaks in concentration some distance from the source, so sharks rely on detecting small delays of less than a second for molecules hitting each nostril. And, that is not all. It seems some sharks can detect smells not only in the water, but also in the air. The oceanic whitetip shark is sometimes seen with its snout in the air. It is thought that it captures air bubbles at the surface and in this way detects an attractive odour, such as a floating whale carcass, long before any other scavenger.

At 25 m (82 ft) in relatively clear water, the shark can spot movements. It can see even in very dim light for sharks, like domestic cats, have a tapetum lucidum, a layer of shiny plates behind the retina at the back of the eye that reflects light back onto the retina's light sensitive cells. It is this layer that is responsible for 'eye-shine', and it ensures the maximum amount of available light falls on the retina, enabling the animal to see almost in the dark. In sharks, the tapetum can be masked. A curtain of melanin-filled cells, known as melanoblasts, migrates into channels that cover the reflective places. Using this, a shark is able to rise rapidly from the dimly lit depths into the bright light of surface waters without being blinded. Not all sharks have the screening; deep-sea sharks have a tapetum but no melanoblasts, an adaptation to a world of inky darkness where the only light is often from bioluminescent fish, including other sharks, and other marine creatures.

BELOW The relatively small eyes of the leopard shark, *Triakis semifasciata*, are typical of a species that is active in bright shallow waters such as the lagoons at Baja California, USA.

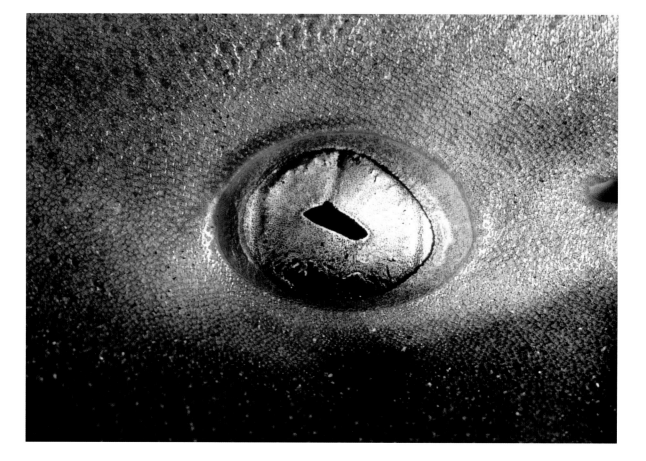

ABOVE The eye of this oceanic whitetip shark, *Carcharhinus longimanus*, is partially covered by a protective nictitating membrane during the last few moments of an attack.

Sharks are generally far-sighted, able to focus from about 25 cm (9 in) to infinity. They focus by moving the eyeball rather than distorting it as in humans. The retina has both rods and cones and so sharks have the capability to see in colour. In some sharks, notably the great white shark, the rod-to-cone ratio is about the same as in humans, giving them acute, bright light, colour vision. They also, have an especially sensitive region, similar to the human fovea, which means the great white can be active at dawn and dusk, and even at night. In some hunters, such as the lemon shark, the sensitive area is a strip across the retina, very similar to that in lions, wildebeest and Thomson's gazelles on the Serengeti. Robert Hueter, of the Mote Marine Laboratory in Sarasota, Florida, revealed the horizontal 'visual streak', and suggests that these sharks have a clear view of the underwater horizon, where prey, potential partners and any danger is likely to appear. In order to protect the eyes while feeding, many sharks have a nictitating membrane, much like an eyelid, that covers the eye. Great whites are different. They swivel the eye back into a cavity, so that nothing can damage them.

Alongside these other senses, the shark's lateral line kicks in, working closely with the auditory system to pick up vibrations and movement of prey. This row of fluid-filled sensory canals on either side of its body and around the head responds to tiny water disturbances and the particle motion component of sound, or near field, so a shark can almost feel the presence and location of something moving in the water. This is a kind of 'touch-at-a-distance', which can pick up stimuli from a hundred metres away or more but which works best within two body lengths, and which enables sharks to manoeuvre even when other senses are unavailable, such as in very murky water.

Recent research by Jelle Atima and colleagues at Boston University, indicates that a shark might use its lateral line and olfactory sensors to track odour plumes in the wake of fish or schools of fish. When fish swim they leave behind a trail of disturbances in the water, like the wake of boat. The pursuing shark could detect these eddies with its lateral line and would be able to smell any fish odours that are trapped within them. In this way, the shark could pursue its prey even in complete darkness.

The most extraordinary sensory system, however, is one that discerns electricity. In the snouts of most sharks are small, jelly-filled pits, known as the ampullae of Lorenzini, and in each pit is a sensor that detects minute electric fields associated with contracting muscles, such as those in a pumping heart or a flexing muscle. The system is remarkably sensitive. A shark is able to detect a change in intensity of a hundred-millionth of a volt per centimetre, the equivalent of a flashlight battery

BELOW Like all fishes, sharks have a lateral-line system that appears as a network of fluid-filled pits containing hair cell receptors around the head and as a line along each side of the body.

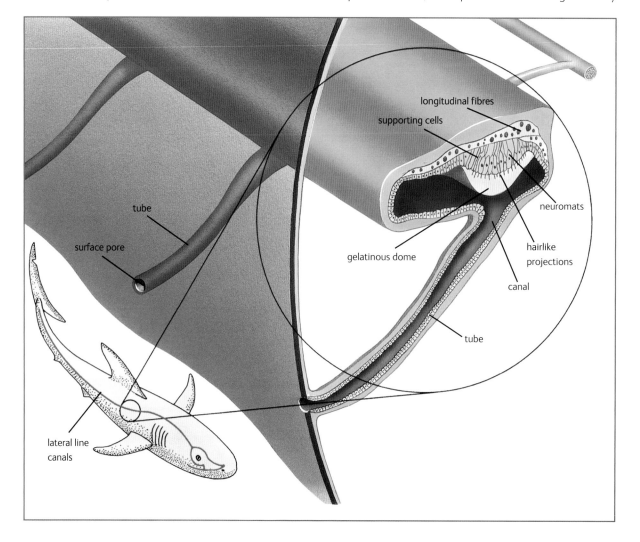

longitudinal fibres

supporting cells

tube

surface pore

neuromats

gelatinous dome

hairlike projections

canal

tube

lateral line canals

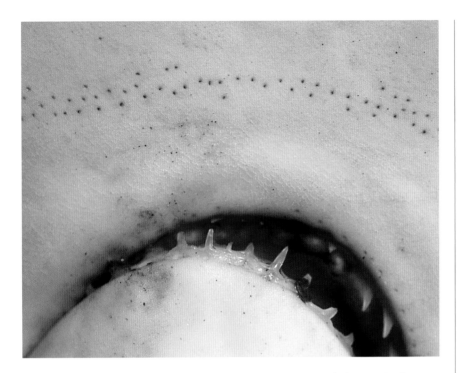

LEFT A close-up of the underside of a hammerhead shark's head shows the spread of the ampullae of Lorenzini, tiny fluid-filled pits containing receptor cells that detect electricity.

creating a field between two electrodes set 1,600 km (1,000 miles) apart. In this way, a shark is able to detect muscular activity in its prey, even if the target is hiding under the sand or gravel of the seabed.

Hammerhead sharks of the genus *Sphyrna* have their electrical sensors, as well as their nasal openings and eyes, spread across the width of their curiously shaped heads. By sweeping its head from side to side, like a person with a metal detector, a hammerhead is able to scan a larger area of the sea floor and more accurately locate buried flatfish, skates or rays. The great white shark uses its electrical sense not for locating prey but in the moment just before contact. In order to protect its eyes from the claws or teeth of seals and sea lions, it swivels them back into special sockets and is effectively swimming blind. The electrical field generated by the seal's muscles guides the shark the last few centimetres to its target. It is also the reason why great whites are seen mouthing or even attacking propellers and shark dive cages. They mistake the electrical field generated by the metal in seawater for muscle activity, but not realizing their error, they continue to do what they are programmed to do – they open their mouths and bite.

Brandon R. Brown, of the University of San Francisco, has been looking at how the ampullae might work and discovered an interesting property. He found that the clear, protein-based jelly is sensitive to temperature fluctuations as small as a tenth of a degree Celsius. It is thought this sensitivity could be used not only to detect the proximity of prey, but also to detect thermal fronts in the ocean where the shark might encounter concentrations of food.

Having taken a bite out of its victim, a shark may then use its sense of taste to determine its palatability. Taste receptors are located on swellings in the mouth and gullet, and it is with these that a shark decides whether to swallow or spit. Great whites tend to spit out human flesh. They prefer animals that are insulated with a thick layer of high-energy fat, and even the most obese amongst us do not have sufficient blubber to interest a great white. So as long as a major artery is not severed and there is not too much loss of blood, some attack victims at least survive an assault by an extremely powerful predator that is quite capable of biting us in half and swallowing the pieces whole.

FOOD AND FEEDING

Generally, sharks are not interested in people as food. While a tiger shark, *Galeocerdo cuvier*, the ocean's garbage collector, will take a chunk out of virtually anything including us, most other sharks prefer to eat fish, squid, crabs and lobsters, sea urchins and marine worms, eating whatever is abundant locally. The diet of populations of smoothhounds of the genus *Mustelus* in Tomales Bay on the US Atlantic coast, for example, is determined by which part of the bay an individual lives. Those near Hogg Island seek out slender crabs and small fish, while others at Indian Beach feast on yellow shore crabs and polychaete worms.

BELOW A blue shark, *Prionace glauca*, employs its integrated sensory system to detect and then feed on a shoal of anchovies near San Diego, on the California coast of the USA.

ABOVE Using its formidable saw-like teeth, a tiger shark, *Galeocerdo cuvier*, cuts up an 'easy' meal of blubber and meat from a floating sperm whale carcass off the coast of Hawaii.

Some shark species have a preference for particular foods. Australia's sicklefin weasel shark, *Hemigaleus microstoma*, is an octopus specialist, while the great hammerhead, *Sphyrna mokarran*, has a penchant for stingrays – and an unusual way of catching them. It pins them down using the side of its head, and then turns rapidly to take a chunk out of the ray's 'wing.' The immobilized ray is unable to escape, so the shark can take leisurely bites out of its quivering body until it has swallowed the lot. One individual hammerhead had 96 stingray barbs stuck in its head, surely a world record.

Many sharks feed at night. Whitetip reef sharks, *Triaenodon obesus*, burst into action in the evening. Protected by their tough skin, they pursue small reef fish through the cracks and crevices of the coral reef, several sharks piling into a hole and scrabbling furiously to extricate the unfortunate victim. An analysis of the stomach contents of blue sharks, *Prionace glauca*, reveals that they contain more food at night, and in the northwest Atlantic a favourite food is pelagic octopuses. They also feast on a variety of fish species, squid, salps and blubber from dead, floating whales.

SOCIAL BEHAVIOUR

When food is concentrated, such as a whale carcass or a tightly packed shoal of fish or squid, many sharks must feed together and, while feeding frenzies (when sharks bite at anything and everything including others of their own kind) have been initiated by artificial feeding, in the wild there is some degree of order amongst diners. There are rules in shark society. Generally, small sharks defer to large sharks, but there is more to it than that.

Great white sharks, for example, were once thought to be solitary nomads but it is now recognized that they can be more social animals showing complex relationships with other individuals. Pairs or small groups of sharks of roughly the same sex and age return to the same area each year. Off the Farallon Island, to the west of San Francisco, two recognizable females, known to local shark researchers as 'The Sisterhood', would always turn up in the same patch of sea each winter to stake out the breeding rookeries of northern elephant seals, *Mirounga angustirostris*, and California sea lions, *Zalophus californianus*. They arrived at the same time, patrolled the same bays and were present at each other's kills. They appeared to communicate not with sounds, as whales and dolphins do, but with a body language of movements and postures.

BELOW A male grey reef shark, *Carcharhinus amblyrhynchos*, (on the left of the illustration) gives its threat display to another male, telling it to 'back-off'. Grey reef sharks will also warn human divers who get too close. If the warning is not heeded the shark will attack.

Great whites will swim parallel to one another or make a carefully timed turn away, probably ways in which they indicate their personal space. They open the mouth and show their teeth in a 'jaw gape', often seen when sharks approach a cage of divers. They use their tails to thwack a rival or splash them at the surface – so-called 'tail-slapping'. And, if a rival fails to back off, the last resort is to make a slashing attack, albeit a low-intensity bite. In fact, it has been suggested that some 'attacks' on humans could be a form of interspecific communication. The shark is not intent on feeding, but uses its sensitive mouth to investigate and ultimately to warn off a perceived rival. The shark bites, causing no more than puncture wounds, in the same way that it would 'talk' to another shark, warning it with a slashing bite.

This behaviour is shown dramatically by another species, the grey reef shark, *Carcharhinus amblyrhynchos*. Grey reef sharks patrol the drop-off into deep water at the edge of coral reefs and atolls, and they have a clear way of expressing their displeasure. When approached too closely, a shark will perform a distinctive threat display accompanied by exaggerated swimming movements. Its back is arched, its pectoral fins point downwards and its snout is raised with its jaws slightly open. It swims in a rather stiff and awkward fashion following a figure-of-eight loop. If the perceived threat fails to back down, the shark then attacks, slashing at the offender with the teeth in its upper jaw. The Galapagos shark, *Carcharhinus galapagensis*, and silky shark, *Carcharhinus falciformis*, perform similar threat displays. The bonnethead, *Sphyrna tiburo*, blacknose shark, *Carcharhinus acronotus*, and great white shark have been seen to adopt the arched body and raised snout posture, but do not swim so erratically as the grey reef shark. These revelations must mean that there is a complete shark body language waiting for researchers to unravel.

One attempt to do so was at Miami Seaquarium, where the behaviour patterns of a group of ten bonnetheads were observed by Sam Gruber and Art Myberg for about six months. During that time, the American scientists were able to identify 18 different movements and postures. Sharks would 'patrol' in a straight line, but 'manoeuvre' in very tight turns. 'Explosive gliding' involved a short but rapid beat of the tail followed by a glide. There were 'head shakes', 'jaw snaps', and 'gill puffs'. The claspers were exercised during 'clasper-flexion' and 'clasper-flexion-thrusts'. In general, sharks within the group were not aggressive to each other, although big sharks tended to be dominant over smaller ones and newcomers were challenged. On some occasions, a resident would go into a 'hunch', during which it raised its head, angled its back, and lowered its tail in a kind of warning, while at other times a newcomer would be greeted with a 'hit' within the first hour of its arrival.

Within the school, sharks would often follow each other. Two sharks moving in a tight circle would be classified as 'circling-head-to-tail', and if the leader turned round abruptly in order to follow, it was described as a 'turn-back'. Three or more sharks moving in a head-to-tail procession was known as 'follow-formation' and sharks manoeuvring to avoid a head-on collision would 'give-way'.

SHARK REPRODUCTION

Baby sharks receive little or no parental care when they enter their perilous underwater world, so shark mothers ensure they receive a good start in life before they are born. Unlike some bony fish that produce millions of eggs and larvae that are left to the mercy of the sea, sharks produce relatively few eggs and embryos, in most species usually less than 100, and protect them well. They do so in one of two ways: by protecting their embryos within egg cases that are deposited somewhere safe or by retaining their embryos inside the body.

The more primitive system is oviparity, meaning 'born from an egg', which is adopted by the dogfish *Scyliorhinus canicula*, the nursehound *Scyliorhinus stellaris*, the swell shark *Cephaloscyllium ventriosum* and the Port Jackson shark *Heterodontus portusjacksoni*. Each of their eggs is encased in a tough capsule, known as a mermaid's purse. The dogfish deposits a translucent, rectangular egg case. Long, curly tendrils at each corner anchor it amongst fronds of seaweeds and prevent it drifting away. The Port Jackson shark's opaque egg case has a spiral flange on the outside. The mother shark is thought to use her mouth to push the capsule into a rock crevice, the flange wedging it firmly in place. The growing embryo inside is dependant totally on the yolk reserves contained within the capsule, and when it is fully developed it breaks out and swims away.

Research with brownbanded bamboo sharks by Blake Harahush, at the University of Queensland, has looked closely at the development of babies from embryo to adult, and found that within their egg cases the embryos develop

their first fins at about 53 days. They are unusually long fins that appear to waft freshwater and oxygen inside the case, and later they morph into the normal fins of a shark. The eyes develop and are ready for use a month before hatching. Why they should appear so early is still a mystery.

In some sharks, such as the spiny dogfish, *Squalus acanthias*, the mother retains less robust egg capsules inside her body where they are even safer from predation or damage, a system known as ovoviparity. The spiny dogfish has five developing embryos, each with its own yolk sac, stacked inside an amber-coloured 'candle' in each of her two uteri. After six months, the outer membrane dissolves or ruptures and the emerging embryos develop for a further 14 months or more. After 20–22 months, one of the longest known gestation periods for any shark, the ten pups emerge head first through the cloacal opening.

Other species are viviparous, meaning live birth. The embryos develop in the uterus or womb and obtain their nourishment directly or indirectly from their mother. A hammerhead shark embryo, for example, relies on a yolk sac for food at first but later the sac begins to grow branches that fasten to the uterine wall, like a placenta, and extract nutrients directly from the mother's blood system. Tiger shark embryos, on the other hand, are fed a kind of creamy 'milk' that is secreted from the walls of the uterus, while mother porbeagles and basking sharks feed unfertilized eggs to their developing embryos. The most bizarre form of viviparity, however, must be that of the sand tiger shark. When the embryos have used up their yolk sac they take to

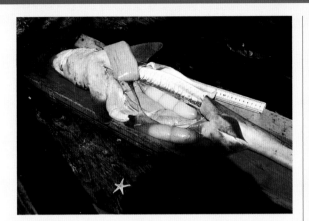

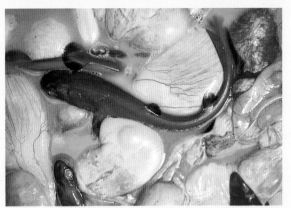

eating each other. Two dominant babies eventually survive, one in each uterus, and they are fed yolk-rich unfertilized eggs until the two intra-uterine cannibals are born.

While in the main, shark mothers leave their newborn offspring to the vagaries of the sea, dusky sharks, *Carcharhinus obscurus*, at least give their youngsters a good start in life. Nigel Hussey, of the University of Bangor in Wales, found that a newborn dusky shark pup has a super-sized liver, about 20% of its bodyweight. It is thought that the enlarged liver buys the pup time when first born, until it catches its first meal. After a few days the liver is reduced to just 6% of bodyweight. However, it means pregnant dusky sharks expend energy and invest it in their offspring's future.

OPPOSITE LEFT The translucent egg case or mermaid's purse of the common dogfish, *Scyliorhinus canicula*, is often found on shores in northwest Europe.

OPPOSITE RIGHT A baby horn shark, *Heterodontus francisci*, breaks out from its spiral-flanged egg case, where it has been nourished by yolk for about seven to nine months.

ABOVE LEFT The dissection of a female spur dogfish, *Squalus acanthias*, shows the tubular 'candles' in which her embryos spend the early stages of their development.

ABOVE RIGHT These deep-sea kitefin shark, *Dalatias licha*, embryos complete with yolk sacs, were found in a garbage bin outside a fish-processing plant in the Azores.

RIGHT A diver off the California coast finds the greenish-amber egg case of a catshark, probably a swell shark, *Cephaloscyllium ventriosum*.

ABOVE In the shallow waters of the Florida Keys, a male nurse shark, *Ginglymostoma cirratum*, grabs a female by the pectoral fin. The bite stimulates the pair to mate.

RIGHT A male nurse shark, *Ginglymostoma cirratum*, inserts one of his claspers into the cloaca of a female during mating in the shallow waters of the Florida Keys.

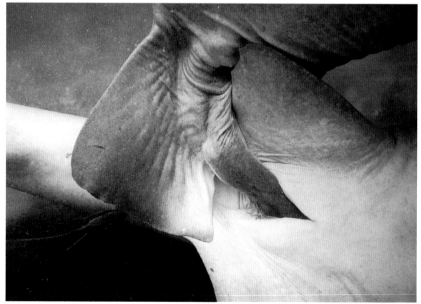

COURTSHIP AND MATING

At some point in their lives, sharks must meet to procreate. Courtship and mating behaviour is rarely observed in the wild, but it is thought receptive females release pheromones, or natural chemical stimulants, into the water to attract males. At Cocos Island, in the eastern Pacific, female whitetip reef sharks have been seen pursued by gangs of eager males.

Mating in sharks can be a violent affair. The male grabs a female by her pectoral fin or the skin behind her head and hangs on tightly. The female's skin is thicker than the male's skin, in some cases as much as three times as thick, so he inflicts less damage. Once he is firmly attached, and the other males have drifted away, he introduces his sperm into her cloaca using one of a pair of sausage-shaped claspers, each a penis-like extension of the pelvic fin. A spur or a bank of terminal ridges at the tip prevents it from slipping out. The sperm is then transferred in a jet of seawater squirted out by a pair of muscular-walled siphon sacs in the male's abdominal wall. Mating complete, male and female part company.

Some sharks, it appears, can dispense with all this. They can switch to reproduce asexually. The revelation came when one of three female hammerhead sharks at Henry Doorly Zoo in Nebraska gave birth without having had any contact with males. DNA analysis at Queens University in Belfast and Nova Southeastern University revealed which mother was responsible, but there was no sign of a father's DNA. Parthenogenesis, as virgin births are known, has been recorded in birds, reptiles and amphibians, but this was the first time in a shark. A second instance occurred at the Virginia Aquarium, where a captive blacktip shark named Tidbit died, but when an autopsy was performed it turned out she was pregnant, and there was no paternal genetic material found in the embryos.

MIGRATION

When males and females go their separate ways, the distance they travel can be considerable. One population of female blue sharks in the North Atlantic, for example, mates off the northeast coast of the USA but then heads out across the Atlantic Ocean, travelling thousands of kilometres to drop their pups on the European side. Even more extraordinary is that many of these impregnated females are immature. They store the sperm until they reach sexual maturity, fertilizing their eggs during the journey. They follow the Gulf Stream and other currents in the clockwise-flowing North Atlantic Gyre while their embryos grow inside, reaching the Atlantic coasts of Spain and Portugal where they give birth. Their next destination is not clear, although females have been seen heading back towards North America, maybe to start the cycle all over again.

Blue sharks are not the only long-distance travellers in the North Atlantic. Shortfin mako sharks also head out across the ocean where they follow warm-water corridors in the ocean. Makos have a preference for sea temperatures between 17 and 22˚C (63–72˚F) and it is this that determines where and when they travel. In summer, they are found all along the US east coast, but come the winter, they head for a 'thermal box' bordered north and south by lines of latitude 20˚ and 40˚ north, to the west by the Gulf Stream, and to the east by the mid-Atlantic ridge. At the centre of the box is the Sargasso Sea, which maintains a mako-friendly 18˚C (64˚F). A tongue of Sargasso water also enters the Caribbean, providing makos with a comfortable thermal corridor to and from the Atlantic, Caribbean and the Gulf of Mexico.

The Gulf of Mexico is the winter destination of several long-distant migrants, including sandbar sharks and tiger sharks. Sandbars have been known to travel from waters around New York and follow the contours of the continental shelf all the way to the western end of the Gulf, a straight-line distance of about 3,250 km (2,019 miles). Tiger sharks make similar journeys. An individual that spent the summer off New York was found six months later about 2,897 km (1,800 miles) away, off the coast of Costa Rica. Tiger sharks, like blue sharks, also cross the Atlantic, with individuals first seen off Florida and North Carolina turning up off the coast of Guinea-Bissau and the Cape Verde Islands.

As an extension of a programme of tagging skate begun in 1974 by Dietrich Burkel of the Glasgow Museum, Scotland, researchers in the northeastern Atlantic have discovered that the tope, *Galeorhinus galeus*, is a long-distance traveller like its larger and more sensational cousins. Female tope tagged in the English Channel have been caught again off the coast of Morocco and in the Mediterranean. It is thought they head south to drop their pups. Similarly, tope on the northwest coast of North America where they are known as soupfin sharks, head south between May and July to drop their pups off the coast of southern California.

The reason researchers know about these epic journeys is that scientists and fishermen have been placing numbered tags, like bird rings, on sharks they have captured, measured and then released. This gives the shark a recognizable 'identity', so when it is caught again it is possible to work out the distance it has travelled and how much it has grown. More recently, sharks are tagged with radio transmitters and the data picked up by satellites in Earth orbit. It means that sharks can be tracked virtually anywhere in the world, at least as long as they come to the surface for the signal to be sent.

Another type of tracking programme involves implanting a radio transmitter inside a shark. The signals are picked up by strategically placed underwater listening stations anchored to the seabed. Every time the shark comes close, its presence is recorded and data about what it has been doing since its last visit downloaded. With this technique, Kim Holland's research team at the Hawaii Institute of Marine Biology has found that tiger sharks migrate around the Hawaiian islands, stopping off where food is seasonally abundant such as turtles arriving or departing from nest sites or the maiden flights of albatross fledglings (see p.67). They also found that some tiger sharks hop off the circuit and keep on going across the Pacific. One individual, a ten-year-old female named 283 was tagged in Hawaii, was caught twice locally, but then was not heard of again until she was caught by fishermen near Cerralbu Island in the Sea of Cortez on the other side of the Pacific, a straight-line distance of about 5,000 km (3,100 miles).

Having discovered that sharks make these extraordinary journeys, the next mystery to solve is how they find their way. The shark's electrical sense is thought to be involved in two ways. Firstly, it is reasoned that a shark should be able to detect the electrical fields produced when tidal and wind-driven currents interact with the vertical component in the Earth's magnetic field. This would give it information about its position on the Earth's surface. Secondly, it might also derive a magnetic compass heading from the electrical field it generates itself when interacting with the horizontal component of the geomagnetic field. If this is true, it means that by using its electrical sense a shark can work out where it is and where it is going.

CHAPTER 2

The world before jaws

T HE ORIGIN OF SHARKS IS EVEN more obscure than that of most other groups of animals, for they have left very little evidence of their existence. Since their skeletons consist of cartilage rather than bone, the only shark fossils we have are those of dermal denticles, teeth, spines and the occasional skeletons, preserved under exceptional circumstances.

The oldest shark-like creatures appeared in the fossil record towards the beginning of the Silurian period, about 450 million years ago. One group, known as the spiny sharks, were not true sharks at all but differed from the early jawless fish in having jaws and bone set in the skin of the gill openings and the 'shoulder' area. They had eyes set well forward on the head and a lateral line system much the same as that of modern sharks. Some spiny sharks, such as *Climatius*, were relatively small – no more than 7.5 cm (3 in) long. They probably gathered in large shoals and were active midwater swimmers.

The earliest known fossil teeth of true sharks appear in the Early Devonian, over 400 million years ago. These teeth are small, no more than 4 mm (0.16 in) across, so their owner may have been no more than 30 cm (12 in) long. Its body might have been long and slender, with a single dorsal fin, paired pectoral fins, a propulsive tail, and covered with small scales. It may have had at least seven pairs of gill slits, and a mouth at the front of its head. This description must be pure speculation, for the skeleton of such a creature, a common ancestor for all the sharks and their relatives, has yet to be found. However, a shark living in brackish estuary waters of early Devonian seas was *Doliodus problematicus*, one of the earliest known sharks. The oldest shark fossil of *Doliodus* was found in Canada in 1997 by Randall Miller and his team from the New Brunswick Museum in Saint John. The 409-million-year-old specimen is 23 cm (9 in) long from snout to upper trunk, and so the entire fish was probably about 50-75 cm (20-30 in) long, about the size of a lake trout, but resembling more a bottom-dwelling angel shark. Parts preserved included the brain case, scales, calcified cartilage, long spines on the pectoral fins and rows of what were probably self-replacing, scissor-like teeth, and all in situ.

OPPOSITE Caught through holes in the ice by the Inuit, the Greenland sleeper shark can be a giant among sharks, reaching 6.4 m (21 ft) long, with claims of a 7.3 m (24 ft) specimen that would rival the great white in size.

BELOW These fossil teeth of an ancient sand tiger shark, *Odontaspis robusta*, were found in Kent, England. Their owner lived in the early Eocene epoch, about 50 million years ago. The slender teeth are from the front of the mouth and the broader-based ones are from the sides.

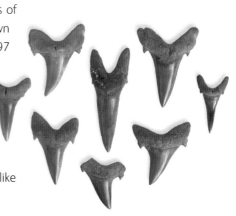

THE AGE OF FISHES

The first major radiation of sharks occurred later in the Devonian period. This was the 'age of fishes'- a time when all fishes, including sharks, diversified greatly. Another one of the earliest true shark skeletons to be found intact was that of *Cladoselache*. It was swimming in an ancient Devonian sea at the time the first amphibians were leaving their footprints on land. *Cladoselache* was no longer than 2 m (6 ft) and torpedo-shaped, with broad-based, triangular fins supported by bars of cartilage. Its dorsal fins were roughly of equal size, and each had a short, stout spine in front. The pectoral fins were relatively large and inflexible, no more than stabilizers, and the pelvic fins small. It had no anal fin, but horizontal keels were present at the base of its tail, similar to those seen in modern mackerel sharks. The caudal, or tail, fin had an unspecialized notochord that turned upwards into its upper lobe, the upper and lower lobes being of equal size – indicating *Cladoselache* was probably a fast swimmer and an inhabitant of the open ocean.

It had large eyes, five pairs of gill slits (not the seven often depicted in drawings) and tough scales around the eyes and at the bases of its fins, but not all over its body. Its mouth was at the tip of its long, slender jaws, rather than underslung like that of many modern sharks. Its teeth were small, sharp and pointed, resembling the dermal denticles found on shark skin, and they would have been used to grab and swallow prey whole.

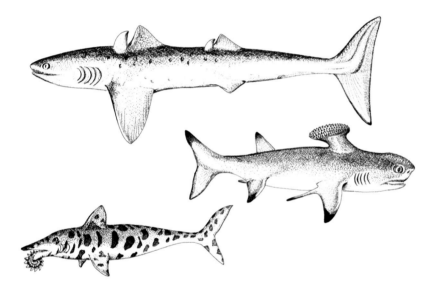

ABOVE While the earliest fossil sharks superficially resembled modern sharks, later species from the 'golden age of sharks' appeared in all manner of curious shapes and sizes. Top, *Cladoselache*; bottom left, *Stethacanthus*; bottom right, *Helicoprion*.

Intact fossils of ray-finned bony fish have been found in the stomachs of some individuals, their orientation indicating that they were taken tail-first, so *Cladoselache* must have been quite capable of out-swimming its prey. It also grubbed about on the seabed. About 25% of specimens so far recovered had been feeding on the blind, shrimp-like crustacean *Convaricaris*, which buried its head in sediments on the sea floor and fed on the dead bodies of fish and squid.

Cladoselache and other sharks living at the time were not alone in those Devonian seas. They would have had to compete with the formidable armour-plated placoderm fishes. Yet, already the sharks had gained a tactical advantage with a body plan that was both simple and hydrodynamically efficient. With a pliable skeleton of cartilage that gave strength without weight, they were better adapted than their rivals and were poised to go on to even greater things.

THE AGE OF SHARKS

By the start of the Carboniferous period, about 360 million years ago, sharks diversified and proliferated to such an extent that scientists have labelled this the 'golden age of sharks'. In addition to the obviously shark-like species, there were some that can only be described as bizarre. The most unusual was *Stethacanthus*. An almost perfect specimen was unearthed at Bearsden, next to a housing estate in the suburbs of Glasgow, Scotland. It probably grew up to 3.4 m (11 ft) long and differed from any other shark, living or dead, in having a helmet of small teeth on its head and a curious structure shaped like a triangular shaving brush sticking out of its back, roughly where its anterior dorsal fin should be. This was topped by dozens of teeth, small ones at the front and larger teeth at the back, and was present in both male and female sharks. Such a conspicuous and awkward structure must have had an important function, but what this could have been can only be speculation. It may have played a role in courtship, had something to do with defence, or maybe it enabled *Stethacanthus* to anchor itself, like a modern remora, to the underside of a larger fish.

Another strange fossil shark, *Falcatus*, was discovered at Bear Gulf, Montana, by Richard Lund of Adelphi University. It was just 14.5 cm (5.7 in) long, and had an L-shaped spine running over the top of its head like a sunshade. Significantly, only males possessed the spine, which was embedded deep in the muscles of the 'shoulder'. As with the 'brush' of *Stethacanthus*, its function remains speculative. Some researchers have suggested the spine was used like deer antlers during male displays of rivalry. Another suggestion is that it served to attract females during some courtship ritual, or had some 'docking' function during mating.

Even more bizarre was the tooth whorl of *Helicoprion*. The shark itself is poorly known, but the pattern of its teeth is instantly recognizable. They formed a whorl, the size of a large dinner plate, erupting from the back of a semi-circular 'conveyor belt arrangement', but the teeth did not fall away at the front as in modern sharks. Instead, they were rotated under the apex of the lower jaw, and then back up into a cavity under the jaw where they were stored in a tight spiral. Why these sharks possessed such a bizarre dental arrangement is another mystery.

There were giants, too, such as the scissor-toothed shark, *Edestus giganteus*. Enormous fossil teeth from such a shark with a mouth a metre (3 ft) wide and a body 6 m (20 ft) long have been found in

BELOW The tooth whorl from the fossil shark *Helicoprion* was at the tip of the lower jaw. The older teeth are at the centre of the whorl, which is about 20 cm (7.8 in) in diameter.

Late Carboniferous deposits in North America. The teeth are replaceable and set in rows, like modern sharks, but old teeth were retained and they protruded in front of the shark's head. With the giant placoderms gone by the end of the Devonian, these enormous sharks with their saw-toothed pinking shears mounted on their snouts would have been the largest vertebrate predators in the sea.

FALLING AND RISING FORTUNES

In the Late Carboniferous period, about 300 million years ago, the period of rapid diversification came to an end, and it seems sharks lived through many millions of years with little evolutionary change. Then, there was a global catastrophe. At the end of the Permian period, about 245 million years ago, extensive volcanic eruptions, together with the resulting climate change and changes in sea level, caused about 96% of marine life to disappear in the greatest mass extinction event of all time – and many of the vanishing species were food for sharks. Most types of sharks, some of which had become victims of their own specialization, joined the casualty list, but a few survived and a second evolutionary jolt caused two main shark groups to fill the vacant ecological niches.

One group included the xenacanth sharks. They appear to have avoided extinction by moving into freshwater. One species, *Xenacanthus*, was a 75 cm (30 in) long, eel-like shark that resembled a modern conger eel. It had a dorsal fin that extended the length of its back and around the tail to join with an unusual double anal fin. Its most conspicuous feature was a single defensive spine growing backwards out of the top of its head.

The other survivors were in the sea. They were the hybodonts, unspecialized sharks that resembled modern sharks but were not their immediate ancestors. Their success demonstrated that the basic shark structure and way of life had evolved successfully tens of millions of years before modern sharks appeared. *Hybodus* was about 1.8–2.4 m (6–8 ft) long and had two dorsal fins, complete with spines at the front, paired pectoral and pelvic fins, and a median anal fin like modern sharks. The paired fins were an improvement on earlier versions in that the bases were narrower and the radial cartilages were often segmented, making them altogether more flexible and free-moving structures.

Hybodus was probably fast enough to pursue prey as well as scour the ocean floor for molluscs and crustaceans. It possessed two types of teeth – pointed grasping ones at the front, and broader crushing ones at the back, like a modern horn shark – indicating a varied diet of small fish, shellfish,

BELOW The belly of this fossil shark, *Hybodus hauffianus*, from Germany shows stains that resemble ink, indicating perhaps that its last meal was of cuttlefish or squid.

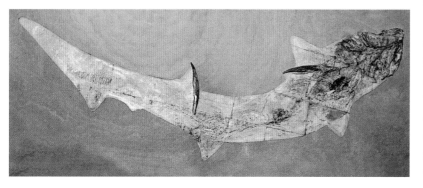

MEGALODON

There was a shark living in the not-too-distant past that was a real giant, dwarfing the biggest great whites and larger even than the whale shark, largest of all living fish. It had a body length and weight of a school bus, jaws lined with 15 cm (6 in) long, triangular, razor-sharp teeth and an enormous mouth that could swallow five adult humans in one gulp. This was the species *Carcharocles (Carcharodon) megalodon*, which resembled the gigantic great white shark, *Carcharodon carcharias*, but was probably not its direct ancestor. It was, however, the most formidable predator ever to have swum in the sea, and one of the most dangerous animals ever to live on the planet.

ABOVE The massive fossil teeth left behind by the gigantic *C. megalodon* dwarf the teeth of a modern great white shark *C. carcharias*, but both have sharp serrations.

Megalodon has long gone. Its fossils are generally found in near-shore deposits, indicating that it probably lived in the coastal regions of warm seas. The profusion of fossils of sea mammals, such as whales and dolphins, in the same rocks suggests there was an abundance of prey for it to feed on.

Megalodon was truly a giant among sharks, reaching its greatest length and size during the Miocene, about 12 million years ago. The largest specimens were estimated to have measured about 16.8 m (55 ft) long, weighed 25 tonnes, and possessed an immense mouth with a gape of about 2 m (6 ft). Some ideas of its shape can be gained from the similarity of its teeth and vertebrae to those of the great white shark, but the sheer size of the teeth, and therefore the powerful muscles needed to open and shut the mouth that contained them, indicates that the jaw itself must have been massive (see also p.48).

Megalodon was not the only representative of its genus. It was just one of a family of enormous sharks known collectively as 'giant-tooths' that resembled living great white and mako sharks. The 'giant-tooths' were undoubtedly some of the largest predatory fishes ever to have lived, but why did they become extinct? Some scientists believe that climate change disrupted the food chains and the plethora of whale and dolphin species on which these huge sharks fed simply disappeared. Others argue that there was plenty of food left. The great baleen whales, including the blue whale, were in the ascendancy and they would have been good to eat and easily killed by these huge, powerful sharks.

Fossil whale remains from the Antarctic, laid down in the sea at about the time Megalodon was in decline, indicate that some of the whales had started to migrate into polar regions, principally, it is thought, for feeding during the summer months much as they do today. Megalodon might have been ill equipped to hunt in these icy waters, and so an impetus for the evolution of the annual whale migration could have been to avoid predation by large sharks. Whatever the reason, Megalodon became extinct about two million years ago.

and crustaceans. The male had hooks on his head (similar to those on modern chimaeras, distant relatives of sharks) that were probably used to grasp the female when mating. Claspers attached to the pelvic fins were used as copulatory organs.

By the start of the Jurassic period, 213 million years ago, the first modern sharks were challenging the hybodonts. These newcomers had more flexible jaws that could be thrust forwards, giving them a distinct advantage in the competition for food. The hybodont lineage began to tail off, and sharks remarkably similar to modern species started to take over.

MODERN SHARKS ARRIVE

The Jurassic and Cretaceous periods were the 'age of reptiles'. In the sea, relatives of the dinosaurs included long-necked plesiosaurs and dolphin-like ichthyosaurs, but the new breed of sharks – streamlined, fast-swimming and equipped with their remarkable battery of senses – were strong competitors. Some were huge. The cretoxyrhinid sharks, for instance, were active hunters over 6 m (20 ft) long and weighing in excess of 1.5 tonnes.

There were also the ptychodonts, a group of sharks known only from their teeth. These were flattened, crushing structures, suitable for tackling hard-bodied creatures, such as ammonites, bivalves and gastropods. Cretaceous deposits also contain the teeth of what look remarkably like those of sand tiger sharks (Family Odontaspididae), and there were the recognizable teeth of large lamnid sharks, relatives of today's mackerel sharks, from species that must have been over 6 m (20 ft) long. Fossil teeth from ancient porbeagles, *Lamna*, for example, have been unearthed in rocks dating back to the Cretaceous.

That sharks arose at all is something of a miracle, for they began to evolve during a series of devastating episodes in the Earth's history that must have had an impact on sharks and their food. At the end of the Triassic period, another 20% of marine families were hit badly by another mass extinction, and at the end of the Jurassic there was another minor event. Then, at the end of the Cretaceous, about 65 million years ago, about 70% of all living things, including the dinosaurs and their relatives, were wiped out. It was an opportunity, however, for others to flourish and some of the new sharks survived the catastrophe. There was a distinct loss of diversity in the groups, but the survivors were a tough, well-honed bunch. These included great filter feeders, such as basking sharks *Cetorhinus*, straining the water for krill in the manner of modern baleen whales; also, tiny fossil teeth, closely resembling those from the mid-water filter-feeding megamouth *Megachasma*, have been found in Tertiary rocks. There were fast-swimming hunters, too, including a new group of sharks that would come to dominate the seas up until the present day. These were the carcharinids – the requiem sharks. These dynamic sharks are found in all warm and temperate seas, in all parts of the ocean: on coral reefs, close to oceanic islands, in the open ocean, in the deep sea and even in freshwater. The most recent family to appear, however, is the hammerheads, with the most bizarre-shaped heads ever to have evolved.

With the demise of the giant reptiles, the mammals began to fill some of the vacated niches, and some returned to the sea. The evolving whales, dolphins, seals and sea cows became the main source of food for one group of sharks in particular – the ancient relatives of the great white shark. The earliest fossil teeth resembling those of modern great whites were found in rocks about 65 million years old. Even at this early date, the great white's ancestors were poised in evolutionary terms to exploit the coming superabundance of blubber and meat, and some species took full advantage, including some of the most powerful predators known to have lived in the sea. Today, the last survivors are the great white shark and its close relatives the makos and porbeagles.

TYPES OF SHARKS

Living sharks can be assigned to eight major groups or orders, each recognized by distinctive external features. These orders can be subdivided into 30 families containing over 460 species, with new families and species being discovered all the time.

No anal fin

Squaliformes
Echinorhinidae
(bramblesharks)

Squalidae
(dogfish sharks)

Oxynotidae
(roughsharks)

Pristiophoriformes
Pristiophoridae
(sawsharks)

Squatiniformes
Squatinidae
(angelsharks)

Anal fin and 5 gill slits

Orectolobiformes
Parascylliidae
(collared carpetsharks)

Brachaeluridae
(blind sharks)

Orectolobidae
(wobbegongs)

Hemiscylliidae
(long-tailed carpetsharks)

Ginglymostomatidae
(nurse sharks)

Stegostomatidae
(zebra shark)

Rhincodontida
(whale shark)

Carchariniformes
Scyliorhinidae
(catsharks)

Proscylliidae
(finback catsharks)

Pseudotriakidae
(false catshark)

Leptochariidae
(barbeled houndshark)

Triakidae
(houndsharks)

Hemigaleidae
(weasel sharks)

Carcharhinidae
(requiem sharks)

Sphyrnidae
(hammerhead sharks)

Lamniformes
Odontaspididae
(sand tiger sharks)

Pseudocarchariidae
(crocodile shark)

Mitsukurinidae
(goblin shark)

Megachasmidae
(megamouth shark)

Alopiidae
(thresher sharks)

Cetorhinidae
(basking shark)

Lamnidae
(mackerel sharks)

Heterodontiformes
Heterodontidae
(bullhead sharks)

Anal fin and 6–7 gill slits

Hexanchiformes
Chlamydoselachidae
(frilled shark)

Hexanchidae
(sixgill and sevengill sharks)

PRIMITIVE DEEP-SEA ODDITIES

There are sharks living today that are similar in shape to those which swam ancient seas millions of years ago. Evolution has not stood still, but these creatures, the so-called 'living fossils', have been in the slow-lane of evolutionary change. They are very similar to sharks found in fossils in rocks laid down up to 250 million years ago, and they all spend time in the deep sea.

GOBLIN SHARK

Browsing through the day's catch at the fish market in Yokohama, Japan, and searching for interesting specimens to sell to the world's museums, an American dealer came across a most peculiar shark. It had a long, flat, dagger-like extension from its forehead and protrusible jaws containing rows of awl-like teeth. The local fishermen called it tenguzame, meaning goblin shark. The year was 1898, and when the scientific paper describing it was published a little later, it became clear that this was not the first time the goblin shark had been brought to the attention of

BELOW This goblin shark, *Mitsukurina owstoni*, with its long, dagger-like snout, was caught off the Japanese coast; here it is being examined by American and Japanese scientists.

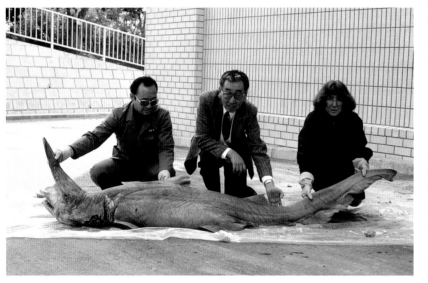

the scientific community. A fossil shark, thought to have been extinct for over 100 million years, and named *Scapanorhyncus*, meaning shovel-nose, had already been described from fossils found in Cretaceous rocks in Syria.

The same creature, now given the name goblin shark, *Mitsukurina owstoni*, appears to have survived for millions of years with little change, and is found today in waters at least 350 m (1,148 ft) deep, where they are thought to feed close to the seabed. The tooth of one individual was discovered embedded in a submarine telephone cable lying in 1,400 m (4,593 ft) of water in the Indian Ocean, off South Africa. Very few goblin sharks have been seen, although catches have been widely spread. Specimens have been hauled up from deep waters off Japan, southeastern Australia, California, Guyana, northeastern Brazil, South Africa, India, Madeira, the Azores, the Iberian Peninsula and the Bay of Biscay, sites that reflect more the presence of flourishing long-line fisheries, such as the black scabbard, *Aphanopus carbo*, fishery off Madeira, rather than offer an accurate distribution pattern for the shark. Indeed, most specimens have been caught on the Japanese coast because of a local long-line fishery. When one is hooked and hauled aboard, it has a pinkish-grey colour with darker fins, and its rather flaccid body seems to indicate a sluggish fish. Its curious snout is covered with electro-receptors, which it probably uses to locate prey in the pitch dark of the deep ocean. Most goblin sharks caught so far have had empty stomachs, but researchers believe they feed on small fish and deep-sea invertebrates, such as ostracods, pelagic octopus and squid. Specimens up to 4.3 m (14 ft) long have since been reported.

The goblin shark is classified in its own family, the Mitsukurinidae, in the order Lamniformes. With its bizarre unicorn-like head shape, resulting from the elongated, dagger-like snout, and its extendible but untidy jaws, this oddity has been described, perhaps unfairly, as the world's ugliest shark.

FRILLED SHARK

The frilled or collar shark, *Chlamydoselachus anguineus*, is another strange species. It is probably the most unshark-like of all sharks. It has the shape of an eel and six frilly gill slits, the first of which almost encircles its body. Its mouth is at the front of the head, rather than underslung, and its teeth are most unusual. It has about 300 small, three-pointed, hook-like teeth set into 27 rows, giving it about 1,000 miniature tridents with which to grasp fish. Its eyes are large and elongated, indicating a deep-water existence. The paired, elongated lobes of its liver account for 25% of its body, giving it almost neutral buoyancy. It has a notochord, a pliable cartilaginous rod that was the precursor to a segmented backbone, and a lateral line in which the long groove, extending along the side of the body and around the head, is not fully enclosed. Longitudinal folds of thickened skin, separated by a groove, run along the underside of its body, but their function is unknown.

BELOW The eel-like frilled shark, *Chlamydoselachus anguineus*, has gill slits with feather-like edges. This specimen was hauled up off the coast of southeast Australia.

Reproductive features have been studied from specimens caught off Japan. Here, scientists have found that there is no breeding season, and eggs at various stages of development are present throughout the year. Only the right ovary is functional, from which three to twelve mature, oval-shaped eggs are produced at any one time. The largest known cells of any living animal, they are each about 10 cm (4 in) across, and protected by a tough keratin capsule. The eggs are retained inside the female's body where the underdeveloped embryos hatch out. Each has external gills and its own sustaining yolk sac. The embryos remain inside for about two years until they can fend for themselves.

Since the first frilled sharks were caught off Japan, they have been hauled up from the depths off Madeira in the eastern Atlantic Ocean; Varanger Fjord, Norway; off Rockall to the west of Scotland; Santa Barbara, California; and off the coasts of Portugal, Spain, Morocco, Namibia, Australia, New Zealand and South Africa indicating a wide distribution in deep water on the continental slope near the coast. The shark probably chases prey amongst rocky reefs and ledges on the steep drop-offs along continental shelves.

A second species is recognized, the southern African frilled shark, *Chlamydoselachus africanus*, for it differs internally from specimens found elsewhere. The internal structure of the cranium and vertebrae, the pectoral fin morphology and intestinal valve twists are different than in other frilled sharks, and it is more than likely that when more taxonomic work is completed more species will emerge.

The shark has an ancient lineage, one of the oldest of all living sharks. Its ancestry can be traced back to at least to the Late Cretaceous, about 95 million years ago, and maybe even earlier in the Late Jurassic about 150 million years ago.

SIXGILLS AND SEVENGILLS

What might be described as a 'monster of the deep' is the broadnose sixgill shark, also known as the cow shark or griset, *Hexanchus griseus*. It grows up to 7.6 m (25 ft) long and lives at depths of over 2,000 m (6,560 ft). It is broad-headed and has a single dorsal fin and a long, flat tail with a small lower lobe. It is uniformly brown above and a lighter buff below, and as its common name suggests, has six gill slits on either side of its body. The teeth in its upper jaw are fang-like and similar to those of modern sharks, but the lower teeth are slanted and comb-like, and altogether more primitive. Its body is covered with three-cusped skin teeth. A conspicuous feature is a pale patch on the top of the head, the so-called 'third eye' that indicates the position of the pineal body, a small ball of light sensitive tissue below the surface of the skin. The function of this organ is probably to detect light from the surface, ensuring the shark is at the correct depth to catch its vertically migrating prey, as well as regulate seasonal changes in its reproductive organs.

The sixgill shark swims slowly and deliberately, approaching food cautiously, but is still capable of a turn of speed to make a capture. The late R. Aidan Martin, director of the ReefQuest Center for Shark Research, told of a sixgill that was seen to pin a ling cod, *Ophio elongates*, to the bottom with its snout and, with its tail nearly

vertical, it spun around and swallowed its prey head first. At the point of contact, a white protective cover slides across each eye. It is shy of light, and specimens kept in captivity for short periods have shown obvious signs of stress when exposed to even low light levels.

Female sixgills are ovoviviparous, with as many as 108 embryos retained inside the mother. Newborn youngsters are about 40–70 cm (16–18 in) long, and juveniles have unusually large dermal denticles along the top of the tail. The large number of pups probably indicates a high mortality rate.

Sixgills are not confined to the deep sea for in summer they enter coastal waters at night off British Columbia and Washington State on North America's west coast, sometimes in water as shallow as 3 m (10 ft). Female sharks often show fresh scars so it is thought they head inshore to mate and later to pup. Young sharks are evident at the same time as the mass spawning of herring and when the salmon runs are in full swing. In winter, when the water clears of plankton, the sharks head back to the deep.

The sixgill shark is found in all the world's oceans including the Mediterranean, and could be the most widely distributed of all sharks. It has been taken regularly by fishermen operating in the Celtic Sea, that part of the Atlantic between southern Ireland and England, and off the west coast of Ireland. Its smaller 2.1 m (7 ft) long relative, the big-eyed sixgill shark, *Hexanchus vitulus*, inhabits shallower and warmer waters off Florida, the Philippines, Madagascar, and the east coast of Africa.

ABOVE The sixgill shark, *Hexanchus griseus*, inhabits the twilight world off the continental slope down to depths of 2,000 m (6,500 ft). This specimen was encountered off the coast of British Colombia, Canada.

ABOVE The broadnose or spotted sevengill shark, *Notorynchus cepedianus*, grows up to 4 m (13 ft) long and, like the sixgill, is found from shallow to moderately deep continental shelf and slope waters.

Members of the same family are the two species of sharpnose sevengill shark, *Heptranchias perlo,* and the broadnosed sevengill shark *Notorynchus cepedianus.* They are also deep-sea inhabitants, but there are reports of them entering shallow-water lagoons on the coasts of tropical West Africa. Most members of the family Hexanchidae are extinct, with recognisable species appearing in the fossil record during the Jurassic period 190 million years ago.

SLEEPER SHARKS

In 1986, another true monster of the deep was seen at the bottom of the San Diego Trough. The crew of the US submersible *Deepstar 4000* was at a depth of 1,129 m (4,000 ft) when a shark swam close by that had 'eyes the size of dinner plates,' according to an eyewitness. It was estimated to be 9.1 m (30 ft) long, and was identified as a Pacific sleeper shark, *Somniosus pacificus.* Its nearest relative in the deep Atlantic is the Greenland or Atlantic sleeper shark, *Somniosus microcephalus.* This species also reaches giant proportions, with lengths reported in excess of 7 m (23 ft). Indeed, in March 2001, a Greenland sleeper measuring exactly 7 m (23 ft) was hauled up by a French fishing boat in the Rockall Trough area of the northeast Atlantic. Another specimen, estimated to be about 6 m (19.7 ft) long, appeared in a video from an unmanned US submersible, the *Nemo,* surveying the wreck of the steamship *Central America* in 1988. The ship went down in waters 2,200 m (7,436 ft) deep, about 440 km (273 miles) southeast of Cape Hatteras, making this species of shark one of the deepest-living species known (only the related

LEFT This Greenland sleeper shark, *Somniosus microcephalus*, was captured through a hole in the sea ice off northern Baffin Island, Canada. The flesh is poisonous and must be boiled three times before eating.

Portuguese shark *Centroscymnus coelolepis* has been found at greater depths). The shark was a male so, as female sharks tend to be considerably larger than males, we can expect some even bigger monsters to be living at the bottom of the Atlantic Ocean.

Sleeper sharks are also among the few sharks to enter polar seas, in both the northern and southern hemispheres. In the north, the Greenland sleeper is thought to venture into northern Russia's White Sea, and frequents the Bering Sea between Russia and North America. In the south, a Pacific sleeper was washed ashore at the Macquarie Island, an Australian dependency in the Pacific Ocean far to the south of New Zealand on the way to Antarctica.

The Greenland sleeper is a sluggish swimmer with a blunt, broad tail, but appears to be an active predator. During the Arctic summer, it comes close to the sea's surface where it is thought to take seals, fish and squid. Every year the shores of Sable Island, Nova Scotia, are littered with seal carcasses sporting mysterious corkscrew wounds that were thought to be caused by Greenland shark attacks, although more recent work in the North Sea ascribed the wounds to seals being sucked into the ducted propellers of ships serving the offshore oil industry.

From September and throughout the winter, Greenland sleepers scavenge all manner of unlikely items from the deep-sea floor, using their highly refined sense of smell to locate carcasses. At one time or another, parts of a horse, an entire reindeer minus horns and a seaman's leg complete with sea boot have been found in the stomachs of sleeper sharks. They also patrol under the Arctic pack ice, venturing into polynyas, which are stretches of open water amongst the ice. They also move into coastal areas around the northern Atlantic in search of polar cod, *Boreogadus saida*, and halibut, *Hippoglossus hippoglossus*.

When a Greenland sleeper travels, it is not alone; it has a strange association with a parasitic copepod *Ommotokoita elongata* that grows to 7 cm (2.75 in) long. The pale yellow creature has two conspicuous egg sacs, and it attaches to the shark's cornea, one on each eye. Researchers think that the copepods may contain luminous bacteria that attract prey to the shark's mouth. There is some circumstantial evidence to support this notion, for many of the fish found in the shark's stomach have no tail, indicating perhaps that it ate them head first.

Although sleepers are generally slow moving, they glide through the water making little body movement and so little hydrodynamic noise, which means they can sneak up on a target without it knowing. As they grow they begin to take on some pretty impressive prey animals, including Pacific giant octopus *Enteroctopus dofleini*, a southern right whale dolphin *Lissodelphis peronii*, southern elephant seals *Mirounga leonine*, giant squid *Architeuthis dux* and colossal squid *Mesonychoteuthis hamiltoni*. Whether these monsters were already dead and the sharks simply scavenged their dead bodies is unknown.

Sleeper sharks are classified in the order Squaliformes, along with dogfishes, cookie-cutters, bramble, rough and lantern sharks.

MEGAMOUTH

On 15th November 1976, the US research vessel *AFB-14* was on station in waters about 4,600 m (15,000 ft) deep, off the Hawaiian island of Oahu. It was about to get underway and the crew were hauling in the two parachute-like sea anchors from a depth of 165 m (540 ft) when something was spotted enveloped in the fabric. Trapped inside one of the chutes was a large shark, 4.46 m (14 ft 7 in) long, but it was no ordinary shark, for this one had great fleshy lips surrounding a broad gape set on protruding jaws. The creature was soon dubbed 'megamouth'.

A group of shark experts examined its dead body, and it was given the scientific name *Megachasma pelagios*, meaning 'yawning mouth of the open sea'. It was a species new to science, and it was a male. There had never been any hint that megamouths existed at all. It was a scientific bolt from the blue.

Since then, according to Henry F. Mollet's detailed listing of megamouths, 49 more have been found at sites all over the world as of June 2010, including off Los Angeles in the eastern Pacific, off Japan and the Philippines, in the western Pacific, Senegal in the eastern Atlantic, Brazil in the southwestern Atlantic, and Western Australia in the eastern Indian Ocean. Most specimens have been dead, either washed up on the shore or caught by fishermen, but a live individual was caught and released off Los Angeles that gave a few clues about the way this remarkable shark lives.

Megamouth is probably a slow-swimming filter feeder. Its skeleton is composed of soft, uncalcified cartilage, its tissues are flabby, and its muscles are thought to be sufficient only for slow, steady swimming. It has large and flexible pectoral fins, a low dorsal fin, and its tail fin is asymmetrical with a greatly elongated upper lobe, indicating a creature that is not in a hurry. Circular weals on the skin indicate it is frequently attacked by cookie-cutter sharks, *Isistius* (see p.102).

RIGHT Caught off Los Angeles, this is the sixth megamouth, *Megachasma pelagios*, to be found, and one of the few to be seen alive. After surviving being towed backwards to port, it had a radio tag attached and was eventually released back into the Pacific.

A radio tag placed on the Los Angeles shark showed that megamouth migrates vertically, following the daily migration of the shrimps and other mid-water fauna on which it feeds. At night, it remains at a depth of about 15 m (50 ft), but by day it descends to about 150 m (500 ft). It feeds on patches of bioluminescent, deep-sea euphausiid shrimps *Thysanopoda pectinata*, pancake sea jellies *Atolla vanhoeffeni* and copepods, and it could be that food is attracted to its great broad mouth by bioluminescent spots around it. The mouth is lined with silvery tissue, dotted with small circular pits, and its jaws are protrusible and can be spread out like a hoop-net. All the shark would need to do is open its mouth and wait for the shrimps to flock in like moths to a flame. Not all experts agree. They suggest that the iridescent silvery lining of its upper jaw could be equally effective at concealing the shark's open mouth when feeding — any prey looking up would not be able to detect megamouth's open mouth against the similar shine of background light. Prey looking down, into the black velvet of the lower jaw, would see only the dark abyss surrounding it. Camouflaged in this way, megamouth could scoop up unsuspecting prey, and there is even the suggestion that it is able to actively suck in prey into its mouth.

Inside the mouth there are many tiny teeth and up to 100 rows in each jaw, each no more than 1.27 cm (0.5 in) high, and the creature has an enormous tongue that almost fills its closed mouth. Its gill-rakers have closely packed finger-like papillae covered by tiny denticles that overlap like tiles on a roof. These filter out the food, and it may be that its round tongue, which is strengthened by an enlarged central cartilage, is used to compress its catch of deep-sea shrimps against the roof of its mouth, in the manner of baleen whales. It would then swallow the resulting food parcel.

DNA analysis by John Morrisey and colleagues from Hofstra University, New York, on the seventh megamouth to be found revealed this shark to be the most primitive living representative of the order Lamniformes. Other tooth and genetic analyses point to a possible Cretaceous origin for these unique sharks.

CHAPTER 3
The great white and relatives

THE ORDER LAMNIFORMES CONTAINS some of the world's most charismatic sharks: the high-profile great white shark, number one in the shark attack league table; the mako, the ocean's fastest shark; the basking shark, the second largest fish in the sea; the sand tiger, a shark that hovers and the thresher shark, the shark with the longest tail.

OPPOSITE The formidable jaws of the great white shark, the world's largest living predatory shark.

HOT SHARKS

The five species of great white, mako and porbeagle sharks that make up the Family Lamnidae are known as mackerel sharks. Although it is unlikely to be the origin of this group name, they share with the mackerel and other fast-swimming fishes, such as tuna, a small horizontal keel at the base of the tail. There is one on each side in the great white and mako, and an additional small keel on each side of the porbeagle's tail. The keel is thought to help the shark turn at speed.

Speed and manoeuvrability are enhanced in these sharks by having muscles that are kept warmer than the surrounding seawater, a feature they share with the closely related thresher sharks. They have a mesh of veins and arteries, known as the *rete mirabile*, or wonderful net, which acts as a heat-exchange system. When warm blood from the muscles passes through this network of parallel arteries and veins, heat is transferred from the veins to the arteries and carried back to the swimming muscles. In this way, body heat is retained, rather than lost to the outside via the gills, and the muscles are maintained about 5°C (9°F) above the temperature of the surrounding seawater. Chemical reactions within the muscle fibres proceed at two to three times the normal rate, enabling the shark to react and move quickly. This ability is enhanced further by having warm eyes, brain and stomach – a great white shark stomach can be up to 13.7°C (24.66°F) above the sea temperature – which ensures these vital organs can work effectively even under changing conditions. Mackerel sharks, therefore, are alert, ready to move rapidly and feed at any time.

BELOW The diagram shows the heat exchange system, or *rete mirabile*, of mackerel sharks. It consists of layers of thick-walled arteries and thin-walled veins sandwiched between blocks of muscle fibres.

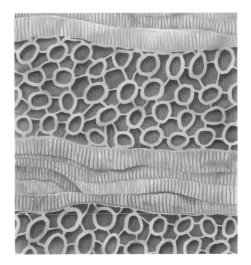

MAKOS AND PORBEAGLES

The fastest known shark is the shortfin mako, *Isurus oxyrinchus*, which lives in temperate and tropical seas worldwide. When hooked by sports anglers, individuals have been seen to leap 6 m (20 ft) clear of the water at speeds estimated to be over 75 km/h (46 mph). Inshore, in the northwest Atlantic, it feeds on fast-swimming fish, such as various species of mackerel, *Scomber* and bluefish, *Pomatomus saltatrix*, while offshore the most common prey are various kinds of squid. It is also quite capable of overtaking swordfish, *Xiphias gladius*, and larger individual sharks have been known to feed on this champion among ocean swimmers: for instance, a 3.7 m (12 ft) long mako, which was caught off New York in 1977, was found to have a 36 kg (80 lb) chunk of swordfish in its stomach.

The shortfin mako is identified by its large eyes, dagger-like teeth and the blue metallic sheen of its body. Its close relative the longfin mako, *Isurus paucus*, lives in deeper waters, and has even bigger eyes, a blunter snout and longer pectoral fins.

Closely related to makos, but of stockier build, are the porbeagles. They grow to 3 m (10 ft) long, and their warm muscles enable them to operate effectively in the colder

BELOW Alert and very active, a fast-swimming shortfin mako, *Isurus oxyrinchus*, appears suddenly off the coast of California.

A STRANGE TAIL

ABOVE The pelagic thresher, *Alopias pelagicus*, is one of three species of thresher sharks. It lives in the Pacific Ocean, and this specimen was seen off the Philippines.

The thresher (or common thresher or fox) shark, *Alopias vulpinus*, is a relative of the mackerel sharks and included with them in the Order Lamniformes. It has warm muscles and eyes, and a warm brain, like the mackerel sharks, but its most obvious feature is its enormous scythe-shaped tail. Individuals up to 6.1 m (20 ft) long have been recorded, of which half the length was tail. To what use this extended caudal fin is put was not totally clear, although there had long been speculation that the shark corrals prey fish into a tight shoal and then disables them by lashing with its tail. It could then gather the dead and dying fish at leisure, behaviour similar to that employed by killer whales off Norway's Lofoten Islands. Evidence has been scant, but sea anglers have reported catching thresher sharks on live baits and long-line fisheries have hauled them in; the sharks hooked not in the mouth but in the tail. However, in May 2010, video evidence from an underwater video camera towed behind a boat off California confirmed that the traditional view of how the thresher catches its prey is indeed true. In the pictures, obtained by Chugey Sepulveda and colleagues from The Pfleger Institute of Environmental Research in Oceanside, fourteen of the of the 33 threshers that chased the bait struck it with their tails with a 65% success rate. The attack was one of two ways: either they swam rapidly forward ending their approach with a tail flick, or they positioned themselves alongside the bait and made a sideways strike with the tail.

There are three species of threshers: the pelagic thresher *A. pelagicus*, with the upper lobe of its tail as long as its body; the big-eyed thresher *A. superciliosus*, a species with enormous eyes that is known to dive down to more than 500 m (1,640 ft); and the more familiar common thresher sometimes caught by anglers in British waters.

parts of the world's oceans where they pursue cold-water fishes, such as species of cod *Gadus*, herring *Clupea*, hake *Merluccius* and haddock *Melanogrammus*. They migrate with the seasons, moving inshore during the summer and to deeper waters for the winter. They sometimes hunt in groups, but they appear not to co-operate; they simply tolerate each other's presence. Populations segregate by age and sometimes by sex. Males predominate off Spain while females are more numerous off Scotland, and immature males are found in the Bristol Channel.

The two species are so similar in appearance that they were not recognized as separate species until 1947. Pacific porbeagles (also known as salmon sharks), *Lamna ditropis*, congregate in large numbers each year at river mouths along the northwest coast of North America and prey on salmon returning to their home rivers to breed. The Atlantic porbeagle, *Lamna nasus*, is rarely seen except when hooked and hauled back to the quayside, where it can be recognized by the shape of its teeth, the angle of the mouth, a second caudal keel (found in no other sharks except its close relative the salmon shark) and a flash of white at the rear of the base of the first dorsal fin.

In the western North Atlantic, Atlantic porbeagles embark on extensive migrations, similar to those in other parts of the world, but here their precise movements are better known. In spring, they head for deeper waters over the continental shelf of Nova Scotia and often as not congregate at thermal fronts where fish have been attracted to concentrations of plankton. In late summer and early autumn, they migrate up to 1,000 km (620 miles) to the shallow waters of the Newfoundland Banks and the Gulf of St Lawrence. By winter pregnant females head south over 2,000 km (1,250 miles) to the Sargasso Sea to pup at depths around 500 m (1,650 ft).

Off the coast of Cornwall in the UK, there are reports of porbeagles engaging in what at first sight resembles play. Individuals have been seen rolling and wrapping themselves in kelp, nudging floating objects, such as driftwood, fishing floats and buoys, and chasing one another. Whether this really is play or some other activity is not known.

GREAT WHITE SHARK

The largest shark in the group, known variously as the great white shark, *Carcharodon carcharias*, man-eater, white pointer (Australia) or blue pointer (South Africa) is unmistakable. Its stout torpedo-shaped body has an irregular but distinct boundary line between the slate-grey to brown topside and the pure white underside. An entirely white shark - an albino - resides in The Fish Collection at Rhodes University, South Africa.

The great white's teeth are evenly triangular and serrated in the top jaw and slightly more pointed in the lower jaw. This powerful predator can grow to an enormous size, although past claims for lengths in excess of 11 m (36 ft) are probably exaggerated. The largest great whites nowadays are more likely to be no more than 5.2 m (17 ft) long with the occasional giant growing to 6.4 m (21 ft), the unconfirmed

length of a great white caught off Cojimar, Cuba, in 1945. As recently as October 2009, however, Queensland authorities warned of a 6 m (20 ft) great white prowling the east coast of Australia, near North Stradbroke Island, after a hooked 3 m (10 ft) white shark revealed two enormous bites on its body.

The great white is a temperate water species, but has been seen in warmer waters, such as the Queensland coast of eastern Australia and around Hawaii. The larger individuals are found most commonly close to seal and sea lion colonies, such as those on the coasts of South Africa, Australia, Chile, Japan, and North America. Here, they use stealth and surprise to catch a seal, approaching mainly from below and behind and then accelerating up towards the target at high speed. They cruise at no more than 3.2 km/h (2 mph), but during an attack can accelerate rapidly to an estimated speed of at least 40 km/h (25 mph). When taking lightweight baby seals off the South African coast, they are not slowed by the impact and, unable to stop, they burst clear of the water in spectacular fashion.

They slam into their larger victims with tremendous force, using their momentum and weight to carve out a large slice of meat and blubber. During an attack, they show five basic jaw movements: the shark first raises its snout and drops its lower

ABOVE The great white shark, *Carcharodon carcharias*, has a dark upper surface and an almost pure white underside, a good example of countershading. Seen from above, it blends in with the greys, blues and greens of the sea, while from below it is camouflaged against the brightly lit surface.

TOP A great white shark, *Carcharadon carcharias*, attacks a bait in the waters off South Africa. It is one of the few sharks that will look above the water surface for potential targets.

MIDDLE A great white shark uses surprise and a sudden burst of speed to take a Cape fur seal, *Arctocephalus pusillus*, near seal colonies on islands off South Africa.

BOTTOM The powerful great white attacks with such energy that it sometimes bursts clear of the water, taking a fatal bite from its victim, which then bleeds to death.

jaw; it then pushes the upper jaw forwards revealing its rows of serrated teeth; on contact, its lower jaw moves forwards and upwards, impaling the prey on the lower teeth so it is held steady for the upper teeth to do the carving; and finally the upper jaw and snout drop as the mouth closes. All this takes place in less than a second. The shark then shakes the forward part of its body from side to side, like a dog, so that its teeth can saw their way through flesh and bone.

The force of the great white's bite is striking. Using a computerised tomography scan of a male shark's head and jaws, researchers in the USA and Australia, led by Steve Wroe of the University of New South Wales, built a working 3-D model and crash tested it with extraordinary results. The largest sharks could have a bite of 1.8 tonnes, compared to a lion with 560 kg (1,235 lb) and humans at 80 kg (176 lb), making the great white one of the hardest biting creatures on the planet. However, for its body size, the great white's bite is not so impressive, but in real terms, and together with the sharp, serrated teeth, it can do a lot of damage. The researchers also tested *Megalodon*, the great white's extinct relative, and came up with a bite of 10.8-18.2 tonnes, three to six times more than *Tyrannosaurs rex*.

If the shark holds its victim in its jaws, it sweeps its tail back and forth in a greater arc than usual in order to push through the water. If the prey is released, the shark returns repeatedly to the floating carcass, taking crescent-shaped bites. If another shark should approach, the original attacker will tilt its body on to one side and slap its tail on the sea's surface. Observers in South Africa have also seen sharks leap out of the water and crash back down on their side, in a display that discourages rivals from feeding on the carcass.

On the US Atlantic coast, seals have all but disappeared, so the sharks have taken to eating harbour porpoises, *Phocoena phocoena*, and the blubber from dead baleen whales, while in the Pacific four sharks were seen consuming a baby grey whale, *Eschrichtius robustus*, off Baja California. Along the California coast Dall's porpoises *Phocoenoides dalli*, Pacific white-sided dolphins *Lagenorhynchus obliquidens*, pygmy sperm whales *Kogia breviceps* and various species of beaked whales (family Ziphiidae) have been taken or scavenged by white sharks. In the Mediterranean, monk seals, *Monachus monachus*, would have fallen prey to great whites, but the seal population has declined hugely due to human disturbance and pollution, so nowadays the larger sharks must turn to hunting swordfish, *Xiphias gladius*, and dolphins, such as Risso's dolphins *Grampus griseus*. Off South Africa, bottlenose dolphins *Tursiops truncatus*, common dolphins *Delphinus delphis* and Indo-Pacific humpback dolphins *Sousa chinensis* are targeted, while off New Zealand dusky dolphins *Lagenorhynchus obscurus* fall prey to great whites.

Great white meals are not confined to sea mammals, however. Skates, rays, bony fish, turtles, crabs, seabirds, squid and other sharks appear on their menu. Young great whites feed mainly on fish, although off South Africa they have been seen to take baby seals. They forgo stealth and surprise and cruise about conspicuously near the seal rookeries. The young seals are such inept swimmers that all a shark needs to do is bob up behind one and snatch it in its open jaws. A few South African sharks have had a go at seabirds, including kelp gulls *Larus dominicanus* and African penguins *Spheniscus demersus* at Deyer Island, but they tend to be random half-hearted attacks.

However, generally, great white sharks appear to plan their attacks. They identify and stake out a suitable site and stick with it. This was the conclusion reached by Neil Hammerchslag and colleagues from the University of Miami, when studying the sharks at Seal Island, off the South African coast. After observing 340 attacks on Cape fur seals, *Arctocephalus pusillus*, during which they recorded the location, depth of water and success rate, they turned over the data to Kim Rosmo, a criminal justice expert at Texas State University's Center for Geospatial Intelligence. Applying the same analytical techniques used in tracking down criminals, they found that the great white shark's attack pattern is very similar to that of a serial killer who returns to the same spot again and again to target their next victim. Smaller sharks, which steer clear of their older and larger cousins, widen their search strategy and are less successful, indicating that some aspects of the great white's predatory behaviour could be learned and then refined by experience.

The sense of smell (the great white has the largest olfactory lobes relative to total brain size of any shark examined so far), sound, vibrations and movements in the water all play a role in tracking down prey, but when closing in on its target the great white shark, like the mako, appears to rely mainly on vision. It is one of the few shark species to 'spyhop', that is, push its head out of the water and look around. This presumably helps it spot seals at haul-out sites or satisfy its curiosity about people in boats. Underwater, a great white can recognize the outline of its target, and it will even attack prey-shaped decoys that emit no scents, sounds, vibrations or electrical fields. Compared to those of most other sharks, its eyes have more cones in the retina, including a dense patch of cones towards the centre, indicating that the great white can probably see with greater definition than most other sharks, and maybe in colour.

Occasionally, however, its senses must let it down. White sharks have been known to attack boats, crab pots, buoys, trawler otter boards and float bags, and they have been found with all manner of objects in their stomachs. Two of the most bizarre records were those of two great white sharks caught in the Adriatic Sea. One contained three overcoats, a raincoat and a driving licence, while the other had an old boot, a plastic bucket, a seaman's oilskin, an intact bottle of Chianti and a cash box containing Yugoslav dinars!

The study of reproduction in the great white shark is rudimentary, due partly to the relative scarcity of the species and partly to the potential danger to researchers. Nevertheless, a picture is beginning to emerge. Males reach sexual maturity when about 3.7 m (12 ft) long, and females at 4.5–5 m (12.6–16.4 ft). The sexes are thought to meet at traditional mating sites, such as the New York Bight, between Cape May and Cape Cod in the northwest Atlantic, and the Sicilian Channel in the Mediterranean. Mating probably takes place in spring and summer, and the resulting embryos develop for about 12 months. A pregnant female might have 5–14 embryos,

LEFT Researchers think that great white shark pups are born in traditional nursery areas. Two probable sites, where juvenile sharks (such as the specimen in this picture) have been caught, are inshore waters on the Atlantic coast of the USA and off the coast of Zanzibar in the Indian Ocean.

which are fed on yolk-rich eggs (oocytes) that are released into the uterus. When close to term, the embryos have functional teeth and these start to drop out and be replaced when the shark is still in the womb. Great white pups have a length at birth of 1.2–1.5 m (3.9–4.9 ft), and they are probably born head first.

At one time the great white was thought to be mainly a coastal species, but we now know they are accomplished long-distance travellers, crossing entire oceans. Along the Californian coast, these sharks appear with unfailing regularity at northern elephant seal and sea lion breeding rookeries at the Farallon Islands to the west of San Francisco, Mexico's Guadalupe Island and mainland sites such as Año Nuevo and Marin Headlands – the so-called 'Red Triangle' (see p.110). When the breeding season is over and the weaned pups have gone to sea, some sharks move out, and scientists from various US research institutes have been tracking them by satellite as part of the TOPP initiative (Tagging of Pacific Predators). They have found that the sharks congregate in a patch of the Pacific Ocean between Baja California and Hawaii, dubbed 'White Shark Café'. The journey takes about 100 days, with the sharks diving periodically to about 900 m (3,000 ft). At the café, they mill about, diving regularly to 300 m (1,000 ft), sometimes as frequently as every ten minutes. Why they stay here and what they are doing on their dives is still a mystery. The area is described as 'a mid-ocean desert'. There has been speculation that this is where they mate, for both males and females arrive in the area, but juveniles turn up too, so other explanations are sought. Some sharks then carry on to Hawaii, perhaps to coincide with humpback whale, *Megaptera novaeangliae*, births there, while most return to the California coast for their annual feast on pinnipeds, each shark returning to its favoured attack site.

HOVER SHARK

A visit to a sizeable marine aquarium will likely bring you face to face with another shark in the order Lamniformes, the sand tiger or ragged tooth sharks, of which there are four species in two genera – *Odontaspis* and *Carcharias*. They look menacing because of the sharp teeth that protrude, even when the mouth is shut, but they are relatively harmless to humans. They are also unusual in having the ability to gulp in air, which is stored in the stomach, enabling them to float motionless in the water. They do this at Cape Hatteras, on the US Atlantic coast, where sand tiger sharks, *Carcharias taurus*, gather in groups of five or six, each shark stacked one on top of another. Both males and females hang motionless in the water until the time comes for them to mate. On the seabed below lie the numerous teeth that have been knocked out when the males grab the females.

In Australia, sand tigers are known as grey nurse sharks. They grow to a length of about 3.5 m (11 ft), and are usually grey or brown grey on the back and white underneath, but an albino was once spotted at South West Rocks off the coast of New South Wales, Australia. They often hide in caves and gullies by day, emerging at night to feed, sometimes in the surf line.

DNA sampling has revealed that the population of great whites in the Pacific are loyal to particular neighbourhoods, those in the southwest not mixing with those in the northeast. However, the study does show that great whites originated from the seas around Australia and New Zealand, and about 200,000 years ago formed a separate group on the other side of the Pacific Ocean.

In the Indian Ocean, great white sharks have been found to make even longer excursions. The shark to make headline news was Nicole, a 3.8 m (12.5 ft) long female. She was tagged on 7 November 2003 at Haibaai, near Dyer Island and Geyser Rock off the South African coast, where sharks feed on Cape fur seals. By 28 February 2004, her satellite tag was recovered from a location 37 km (23 miles) south of Exmouth Gulf, Western Australia. She had travelled 11,000 km (6,835 miles) in 99 days; but there was more to come. Nicole was well known to scientists studying great whites off South Africa, and on 20 August 2004 her distinctive dorsal fin was spotted back at Dyer Island. It was the first evidence of an inter-continental, trans-oceanic return migration for great white sharks.

BASKING SHARK

Most shark species are active hunters or scavengers, but the really gigantic sharks are gentle, harmless filter feeders. The basking shark, *Cetorhinus maximus*, is the world's second biggest fish, after the whale shark (see p.98). The largest accurately measured specimen was trapped in a herring net in the Bay of Fundy, Canada, in 1851. It was reported to be 12.27 m (40 ft 3 in) long and weighed an estimated 16 tonnes. This specimen was exceptional. More usually, mature basking sharks average 7.9 m (26 ft). The biggest baskers are the females and they come to the surface when the plankton blooms. Males seem to swim deeper, coming to the surface only to mate. Both males and females are easily recognized by the enormous dorsal fin, the stout, sometimes bulbous, snout, and the enormous gill slits on each side of the body that almost meet on the dorsal surface. A basking shark has many tiny hooked teeth about 5 mm (0.2 in) high, arranged in 6 rows in the upper jaw and 9 in the lower, with a hundred teeth in each row. The animal's skin is covered by tiny, backward-facing dermal denticles and these are bathed in a thick, black, foul-smelling mucus. Circular wounds are thought to be the work of parasitic sea lampreys, *Petromyzon marinus*. The body colour has been variously described as dark grey to dusky brown.

Oil from the basking shark's enormous liver was once used to fuel the early oil lamps of New England. In the Second World War it was used to lubricate high-flying aircraft, and more recently has been used in cosmetics. For the shark, it could be a means of storing food to enable it to live through the leaner times of winter.

Like the whale shark, the basking shark is a filter feeder. A large basker can plough through the surface waters with its metre-wide (3.3 ft wide) mouth agape at about 3–5 km/h (1.9–3 mph), processing up to 7,000 litres (1,540 gallons) of seawater an hour. It sieves the water using enormous gill rakers (long processes of the gill arches), evolved to support a high flow rate. These huge comb-like structures filter out the tiny free-floating larvae of molluscs and crustaceans, such as crabs and lobsters, as well as the other constituents of the zooplankton, such as fish eggs, copepods, and cirripedes (barnacles). When it has sieved enough food, the great shark closes its cavernous mouth and swallows the accumulated mass in one enormous gulp.

BELOW Basking sharks, *Cetorhinus maximus*, can be seen feeding close to the shore in temperate seas worldwide during the summer months.

ABOVE One of several large basking sharks, *Cetorhinus maximus*, feeding off California, opens its huge mouth to filter out plankton that concentrates in surface waters during the spring and summer.

Basking sharks are seen mainly in cold and warm temperate coastal and continental shelf waters, off the coasts of North and South America, Australia, New Zealand, and Japan, as well as the British Isles and Europe. They are found in the Mediterranean, and also move into the tropics. In temperate regions, they are generally observed in spring and summer, disappearing from view in winter. Until recently, their winter hideouts have been a mystery but satellite tagging of basking sharks off Massachusetts in the northwest Atlantic, by Gregory Skomal and colleagues from the Massachusetts Division of Marine Fisheries at Oak Bluff, is beginning to fill in the picture. The data from 18 tagged sharks revealed that although eight hung around the eastern seaboard of North America, the other ten travelled great distances – to Bermuda, Puerto Rica, the Caribbean Sea and even to the mouth of the Amazon in Brazil, diving to depths of 1,000 m (3,300 ft) during their journeys, which would explain why nobody has seen them.

Around the British coast, where much research has been carried out, baskers are present in spring and summer, with a high concentration off the southwest of England, the Isle of Man, and the Firth of Clyde. The first individuals are seen in early spring in the English Channel, while later in the season they are found progressively northwards along the west coast of Britain. The early sharks travel and feed in groups of 3–6 individuals, with the occasional loner, and are all under 4 m (13 ft) in length. The larger, sexually mature adults come along later. All are travelling in a definite direction, although where from and where to is still a mystery. On occasions, the English Channel can be thick with these sharks. In 1994, for instance, about 50 or so basking sharks were spotted off The Lizard, the southernmost part of mainland Britain, and in mid-May 1998, more than 500 individuals suddenly appeared in the same area. The school was so dense that fishing boats headed for port in case they were damaged or capsized.

A similar event took place in the Irish Sea in June 1989. During a period of hot, still weather three huge schools of basking sharks came close to the west coast of the Isle of Man, where one group of more than 50 sharks entered the harbour at Peel and came to within a few feet of the shore. The sharks were accompanied by millions of jellyfish, a patrolling thresher shark, and a number of the small sharks called tope, *Galeorhinus galeus*. The schools were spread out over a 15 km (9 mile) stretch of sea, and contained sharks of both sexes and all sizes, the large females estimated by local fishermen to be 6–7.5 m (20–25 ft) long. One giant was spotted by an observer in a microlite aircraft and was thought to be a submarine at first. When it swam beside a 12 m (40 ft) long ketch, it was seen to be about the same length, which would make it a similar length to the giant Bay of Fundy shark.

Throughout their visit, the sharks were actively feeding, their large gaping mouths clearly visible, slowly opening and closing to sieve plankton from the warm surface waters. Baskers often feed in the numerous eddies caused by the rise and fall of the tides. These are recognized at the surface by the concentrations of seaweed under which the sharks feed. They also seek out thermal fronts between currents in the sea and other areas of the sea, and junctions, such as the rip-tides off headlands, where plankton, seaweeds, and human flotsam and jetsam is concentrated.

At one time it was thought that these giants encountered plankton swarms randomly, but David Sims, of the Marine Biological Association in Plymouth, has found that they are selective filter feeders that seek out the most productive plankton patches. They forage along the thermal fronts and 'actively select areas that contain high densities of large zooplankton', especially large calanoid copepods such as *Calanus helgolandicus* and less of smaller forms. They remain with a patch for up to 27 hours, and move between patches during the course of 1-2 days.

In the southwest of England, where the study was carried out, the basking sharks were found in well mixed, cool waters along a boundary about 8 km (5 miles) offshore, separating inshore coastal waters from stratified waters on the north side of the English Channel. What attracts the sharks to the plankton patches is unclear, although there is speculation that either their electroreceptors in the snout pick up the muscle activity of the copepods or their olfactory sensors detect the odour of dimethyl sulphide, which is produced by phytoplankton being grazed by zooplankton, and which is used as a foraging cue by certain seabirds. Whatever the cue, basking sharks were not the only animals to find the plankton swarms. Mackerel *Scomber scombrus*, whiting *Merlangius merlangus* and grey mullet *Chelon labrosus* were often feeding on the zooplankton in the sea ahead of the sharks, along with northern gannets, *Sula bassana*, that were, in turn, feeding on the fish.

RIGHT The large dorsal fin, snout and tail of a basking shark pushing out of the sea's surface could be mistaken for a sea serpent. Some shark researchers think that many of the mysterious sightings, claimed as evidence of unknown monsters, could be attributed to basking shark activity.

During the 1989 event, observers also spotted what they considered courtship behaviour. They watched small groups of sharks swimming nose-to-tail in circles. One 11 m (36 ft) long individual, probably a female, with a conspicuous large white dorsal fin, was followed by three smaller sharks, which repeatedly moved alongside and rolled with her. It is thought the male basker grasps the female's pectoral fin in its mouth, in the manner of most other sharks.

Pregnant basking sharks are rarely caught, so the period of gestation and the way in which the embryo develops must be pure speculation. The babies are thought to grow in the uterus for over a year, where eggs produced by their mother nourish them. They emerge when they have reached a length of about 1.8 m (6 ft).

Close to the Isle of Man, observers also witnessed breaching. Basking sharks breach, like whales and great white sharks, but it is not clear why. The underside of their heads are festooned with sea lampreys, and these tenacious parasites clasp on to the softer underside of sharks with tooth-filled, circular mouths and rasp away the skin in order to suck on the blood. The spectacular leaps could be a way to dislodge them.

Later in the season, the sharks appear off the west coast of Scotland, but in September they simply disappear. Where they go in the northeast Atlantic has been a mystery, although there are several theories and research is beginning to reveal at least some parts of the story. One suggestion is that they head south to places where plankton is still abundant during the winter, returning when conditions are favourable the following spring. Another theory proposed they 'hibernate' in deep water, not far from their summer feeding grounds, sitting out the winter on the seabed where they moult their gill rakers. This view was fuelled by the fact that basking sharks have smaller livers at the end of winter than at the end of summer, suggesting they were not feeding, but recent research shows that they do, indeed, shed their gill rakers and grow new ones, but that it is a continuous process. They do not shed them all at once.

A third proposal has them heading for deeper waters in winter, as do many other species of sharks, and switching to feeding on mid-water organisms that migrate to the surface each night. This is the favoured view today, for David Sims' studies show that baskers are active all year and in winter spend time at depths of 900 m (3,000 ft), travelling thousands of kilometres while tracking plankton blooms at the surface and in the depths.

As with whale sharks, it was once thought that basking sharks lived in discrete populations in different parts of the ocean, but a tracking study led by Mauvis Gore, of the University Marine Biological Station on the Isle of Cumbrae, discovered that in the summer of 2007 one large, mature female swam 9,589 km (5,958 miles) from the Irish Sea across the Atlantic to Newfoundland. En route, she followed the daily vertical (diel) migration of organisms to the surface at night and into the depths during the day, and the shark dived to a record 1,264 m (4,147 ft). It was also the first evidence of a link between European and North America stocks, and a trans-oceanic journey comparable to great white shark excursions between South Africa and Australia (see p.58) and California and Hawaii (see p.57). Why the shark should make such a journey is unknown, although basking shark courtship behaviour has been witnessed off Nova Scotia, as well as in British waters.

The basking shark is included in the order Lamniformes, along with great whites, porbeagles, makos, sand tigers, threshers, megamouth, crocodile and goblin sharks, and is the only extant member of the family Cetorhinidae.

CHAPTER 4

Requiem sharks and hammerheads

D IVE ON ANY TROPICAL CORAL REEF and you are sure to encounter at least one species of requiem shark, but hammerheads (apart from the formidable great hammerhead) tend to be rather more flighty. Both groups are included in the order Carcharhiniformes, the largest order of living sharks, with 8 families and 50 genera currently recognised (although taxonomists could be moving towards 14 families and 60 genera). They are also known collectively as 'ground or whaler sharks', and include the only sharks to live regularly in freshwater habitats.

REQUIEM SHARKS

The requiem or carcharhinid shark family is the most recent to have evolved, and today its members dominate the oceans. Most are streamlined hunters with a torpedo-shaped body, prominent triangular dorsal fin, a tail with the upper lobe larger than the lower, powerful jaws, and a mouth filled with very effective teeth. These sharks range in size from 0.9 m (3 ft) to 6.1 m (20 ft) long. Many have markings such as white or black tips or edges to the fins that are thought to be visual species-recognition signals.

TIGER SHARK

The largest and most notorious of the requiem sharks is the tiger shark, *Galeocerdo cuvier*. It can be a huge and powerful fish, and as number two in the shark attack league table (after the great white shark), it is considered highly dangerous to people. Easily identified by the broad, square head, faint stripes on the body (appearing as stronger blotches on juveniles), lateral keel, unusually long upper tail lobe, and distinctive saw-shaped, hooked teeth in the upper and lower jaw, the tiger shark is one of the most feared sharks in the world. It ranges widely, with a record of one off Iceland, but is more usually found in the tropics and sub-tropics.

BELOW Baby tiger sharks, *Galeorcerdo cuvier*, have blotches rather than stripes. This youngster at Bimini in the Bahamas cannot be more than a few days old.

ABOVE This adult tiger shark in the Indian Ocean off South Africa is a powerfully built creature. The species gets its common name from the way in which its juvenile blotches coalesce to form a pattern of tiger stripes.

Although tiger sharks encountered today are generally no longer than 4 m (13 ft), individual sharks have been known to grow even larger. The longest accurately measured tiger shark was trapped in a shark net at Newcastle, New South Wales, in 1954. It was 5.5 m (18 ft) long, and weighed 3,360 kg (7,407 lb). It is likely that even larger individuals are swimming in the oceans. In 1957, for example, a gigantic female, which was claimed to be 7.4 m (24 ft) long but not confirmed, was caught off the coast of Indo-China.

Little is known about tiger shark biology, for although this species is commonly caught by anglers and commercial long-line fishing vessels, it is not particularly abundant in any one place. Surfers and bathers in Hawaii and other islands in the Pacific Ocean might disagree after spates of attacks during recent years, but humans are among an extremely mixed bag of items consumed. According to popular accounts, the tiger shark is credited with eating all manner of bizarre foods. At one time or another, rubber tyres, a roll of tar paper, a roll of chicken wire, a bag of potatoes, a sack of coal, beer bottles, plastic bags, a tom-tom drum, pork chops, hamburgers, lobsters, pants, horns of a deer, cloth rags, glass bottles, leather shoes, tennis shoes, sea snakes, squid, unopened tins of green peas and salmon, cigarette tins, the metal casing of an artillery shell, a bag of money, explosives, pet cats and dogs, parts of dolphins, porpoises and whales, other sharks,

BIRDS ON THE MENU

Ever alert to a feeding opportunity, tiger sharks appear with unbelievable regularity along the shores of the westerly 'low islands' in the Hawaiian chain, where the local populations of fledgling Laysan albatrosses, *Diomedea immutabilis*, and black-footed albatrosses, *Phoebastria nigripes*, are ready to take their first flight. How the sharks know when to congregate, and how they 'remember' the annual event is a mystery. The albatross fledglings practice their takeoffs on the beach, but eventually they must take to the air and fly across the sea. The tiger sharks are waiting. A novice flyer might put down for a rest on the sea's surface, but it is quite likely to find a tiger shark pushing its nose out of the water and trying to pull it below. The chick has an evens-chance of escape, however, for the shark is manoeuvring in very shallow water, unable to dive down and grab the prey from below, and the buoyant bird is often pushed away from the shark's mouth by the pressure wave ahead of its snout and is able to flap back into the air.

During the course of the season, however, the sharks have been seen to adopt a new technique. Instead of attempting to attack from below and behind, a shark will leap clear of the water, rush across the surface, and land open-mouthed on the unfortunate victim. The bird then has absolutely no chance of getting away. Whether the sharks have 'learned' to change their feeding method, or whether observers are watching a different bunch of sharks that have already mastered the technique, the previous ones having moved on, is a matter for speculation.

LEFT A tiger shark seizes a young black-footed albatross, *Phoebastria nigripes*, at French Frigate Shoals, Hawaii.

sting rays, and a variety of land and sea birds have been found in the stomachs of tiger sharks. Nevertheless, the tiger shark is not considered to be an indiscriminate eater. It is more an eager opportunist and inveterate scavenger – the ocean's dustbin with fins.

It is often said to feed mainly at night, but reports from around the world suggest that it feeds at any time. There appears to be a daily pattern of movement from deep waters, where they have been tracked to 335 m (1,100 ft), by day to coastal waters at night. It was once thought that they were loyal to a particular feeding site, but now we know they rarely stay in one place for long, but keep moving on. The tiger shark's powerful slicing teeth can cut through the shells of sea turtles, and where they are abundant, the tiger shark is probably an important predator. Intact flippers and fragments of turtle shells have been found in tiger shark stomachs, and these indigestible items are ejected by turning the stomach inside out and pushing it through the mouth, an ability the tiger shark shares with many other species of sharks.

BULL SHARK

The bull (or cub) shark, *Carcharhinus leucas*, is number three in the shark attack league table, although some experts suggest it should be considered for the top spot. It is thought to have been responsible for many attacks on humans attributed to other sharks, including great whites, particularly in warmer waters. It has a heavily built body, broad pectoral fins with pointed tips, a blunt snout, small round eyes, large and powerful jaws, triangular-shaped teeth with coarse serrations in the upper jaw, and dagger-like teeth in the lower jaw. The upper surface of the body is grey, and the edges of the fins are dark in younger specimens.

The bull shark is a first-class hunter with refined senses, including the ability to hear sounds in the 100–1500 Hz range, the middle part of the spectrum of human hearing. It cruises relatively slowly but it can put on an extraordinary burst of speed when homing in on a target. It regularly takes all manner of prey, including bony fish, other sharks, skates and rays, crustaceans, molluscs and seabirds, and occasionally feeds on dolphins and sea turtles. The bull shark also turns up at shark pupping grounds, such as the sandbar shark, *Carcharhinus plumbeus*, nurseries along the

BELOW The voracious bull shark, *Carcharhinus leucas*, frequently preys on young sharks. This individual in the Bahamas is on the lookout for baby lemon sharks.

northern coasts of the Gulf of Mexico, where it is a voracious predator of baby sharks. The remains of antelope, cattle, rats, dogs and even pieces of hippopotamus found in bull shark stomachs betray its habit of invading freshwaters.

The bull shark enters large rivers and is sometimes encountered many kilometres from the sea. Individuals have been seen over 3,200 km (2,000 miles) upriver from the mouth of the Amazon and 550 km (342 miles) from the sea in the Zambezi River. In the Ganges, they are most probably responsible for attacks on pilgrims that were formerly attributed to another requiem shark, the Ganges shark, *Glyphis gangeticus*. Bull sharks have also been known to enter the Hooghly River in India, the Perak River in Malaysia, the Congo, Gambia, Limpopo and Umgeni in Africa, the Tigris and Euphrates of Iraq, the Rewa River on Suva in the Fiji islands group, the Atchafalaya and Mississippi Rivers of North America, and the Brisbane River in Queensland, Australia, where smaller individuals have been seen to leap clear of the water and spin in the air. The behaviour is baffling to fishermen and scientists alike.

This shark is also found in lakes, where it is thought not to be a permanent freshwater resident, but appears to migrate via connecting rivers between sea and lake. Lake Jamoer and Lake Santini in New Guinea and Lake Izbal in Guatemala are known shark lakes, although the most famous is Lake Nicaragua in Central America. Here the sharks enter and leave the lake by the Rio San Juan, negotiating rapids and other natural barriers like salmon to travel the 100 km (62 miles) to and from the Caribbean Sea. They are able to enter freshwater by retaining salts. The kidneys and a salt gland near the tail help recycle salts. Without this adaptation, they would take in too much water because of the natural process of osmosis and their cells would rupture.

It is thought the main reason for entering lakes, rivers and estuaries is to drop pups in a relatively safe environment. Generally, near-term females and juveniles enter fresh and brackish waters. Pregnant bull sharks in the Florida area, for example, seek out traditional pupping sites, such as the shallow lagoons of the Indian River, where they drop their pups and quickly return to the sea. The youngsters are left behind, where they feed on catfish and stingrays, relatively safe from the predatory attention of other sharks. Similarly, the Mississippi Delta in the USA and the Brisbane River in Australia are known pupping grounds for bull sharks.

Females usually give birth to 5–6 pups, although up to 13 have been known. Each is about 75 cm (30 in) when born. They grow slowly and do not reach sexual maturity until 15–18 years old, when they are about 2 m (6.6 ft) long. Bull sharks can live to 25 or more years, but large specimens rarely grow bigger than 3.5 m (11 ft 6 in) long.

OCEANIC WHITETIP SHARK

Small eyes indicate that the oceanic whitetip shark, *Carcharhinus longimanus*, is a surface-living, open-ocean species. It can be recognized instantly by its large, rounded, spade-like anterior dorsal fin and long pectoral fins that are mottled white at the tip. Body colour seems to vary with location: those close to Hawaii in the Pacific Ocean have a beige back, oceanic whitetips on the Indian Ocean generally have grey backs, while in the Red Sea their backs are brown.

RIGHT An oceanic whitetip shark, *Carcharhinus longimanus*, passes close to Big Island, Hawaii. Recent research indicates that, as with other sharks that ply surface waters, when its dorsal fin cuts through the sea's surface it could be detecting pressure waves associated with activity nearby, such as a struggling animal.

It is one of the larger requiem sharks, with mature fish reaching up to 4 m (13 ft) long. Unlike most other shark species, it lives permanently in the open ocean in waters off continental shelves where the water temperature is above 21 C (70 F). If it drops below 18 C (64 F) the sharks move away, so it is a mystery how one came to be washed up at Gullsmarsfjorden on Sweden's west coast in September 2009.

In its normal environment, it is the shark most likely to arrive at the scene of mid-ocean air or sea disasters, and is therefore potentially dangerous to people. Like many sharks it is an opportunist, and being an open-ocean species it must take advantage of any and every opportunity to feed. It will, for example, follow pods of pregnant sperm whales, waiting for the time of birth and the inevitable bounty of nutritious afterbirths. It can be expected to appear also at whale carcasses floating at the sea's surface. It is often seen in association with other marine creatures. US researchers reported seeing a group of oceanic whitetips accompanied by dolphin fish, *Coryphaena hippurus*, eight to ten fish swimming to the rear or to one side of each shark. Off Hawaii, they have been seen to tag along with shortfin pilot whales, *Globicephala macrorhynchus*; researchers think the sharks follow the whales when they locate shoals of squid at depth.

In the past, oceanic whitetips have been seen in very large groups. In June 1941, for example, the crew of the research vessel *Atlantis* reported seeing a school containing many hundreds of sharks about 80 km (50 miles) off the Massachusetts coast. According to deep-sea fishermen, the further from land they are seen, the more numerous they become, and they are often spotted following ships at sea. When attracted to something resembling food, they move in immediately, unlike other open water sharks, which tend to swim around cautiously in decreasing circles before an attack. Underwater pioneer Jacques-Yves Cousteau described them as 'the most dangerous of all sharks'.

Because the oceanic whitetip is a species of the open ocean, where research is relatively limited, little is known about its general biology and reproduction. Females are thought to head for nursery areas on the equator, where pregnant sharks drop between six and nine pups, each about 75 cm (2.5 ft) long. Growth is unusually rapid, young sharks reaching sexual maturity in just a little over two years.

BLUE SHARK

The blue shark, *Prionace glauca*, is considered by some shark watchers to be the most beautiful of all the sharks. It has a slim, streamlined body and blue or indigo-coloured skin above. Other distinctive features are the long, pointed snout, large eyes with the black pupil surrounded by a white ring, and long, wing-like pectoral fins. The

BELOW A blue shark, *Prionace glauca*, feeds on a shoal of market squid, *Loligo opalescens*, that congregates annually off the California coast to mate.

blue shark is found all over the world in temperate, sub-tropical and tropical seas, cruising mainly near the surface in higher latitudes and diving into deeper waters closer to the equator. It can be found in packs of a hundred or more individuals, and was one of the commonest sharks in the ocean, although nowadays the shark fin soup industry has taken its toll (see pp.114–115). Adult sharks grow to a maximum length of about 3.8 m (13 ft), although Pacific blues rarely exceed 1.8 m (6 ft). The largest accurately measured specimen was 3.84 m (12 ft 7 in) long.

The blue shark feeds mainly at night. Its stomach contents include a variety of fish species, squid, pelagic octopus, and salps. Schooling fish dominate the menu inshore and squid offshore. In order to catch these fast, agile prey it is able to accelerate rapidly, and in laboratory tests it has reached speeds up to 70 km/h (44 mph) for brief periods. The blue shark will take starfish from the seabed and seabirds from the surface, as well as scavenging

ABOVE With long, narrow, wing-like pectoral fins and a super-slim body, the blue shark, *Prionace glauca*, is perfectly shaped for long-distance journeys across all the world's tropical and temperate seas.

the blubber from dead whales, tearing off 9 kg (20 lb) chunks in each mouthful. Whatever the prey, it takes full advantage of anything that is seasonally abundant. At Santa Catalina Island, off the California coast west of Los Angeles, blue sharks feed on swarms of mating and spawning market squid, *Loligo opalescens*. The sharks plough through the shoals with their mouths agape, swinging their heads from side-to-side. They are such enthusiastic eaters that they gorge themselves, regurgitate their stomach contents and then start the feast all over again.

Blue sharks are great ocean travellers, riding the ocean currents and covering an estimated 37 km (23 miles) a day. As they swim, they make frequent, vertical excursions between the surface and the depths down to several hundred metres. They dive at an angle of 5–19° to the horizontal and move through waters of different temperatures, sometimes passing through a 20°C (68°F) change in just six minutes. The reason is unclear: it could be a way of being in the right place at the right time in order to intercept vertically migrating prey, such as open-water octopus and squid. Alternatively, it could be a way of detecting the odours of prey that have spread out horizontally in different layers at different depths. By swimming up and down through the layers the sharks have a better chance of detecting something to eat. It could also be that the sharks adopt a swim-glide method of propulsion, an energy saving system for long-distance travel; or it could be a means of regulating body temperature by moving periodically from the cold depths, to which they dive to catch squid, to the surface to warm up.

There is also another explanation that is gaining credibility. The vertical movement might be a way of checking magnetic bearings from the magnetic disposition of the rocks on the sea floor, and from seamounts and other anomalies. The sharks may find their way using magnetic beacons on the sea floor (see also p.88).

LEMON SHARK

The lemon shark, *Negaprion brevirostris*, gets its name from the hint of yellow in the colour of its skin. It is a temperate and tropical, shallow-water species, stoutly built, and armed with narrow fish-grabbing teeth. It grows to a maximum of 3.4 m (11 ft) long, and can be recognized by its two dorsal fins of almost equal size. It can survive in extreme conditions, including high water temperatures, up to 30°C (86°F), and low oxygen content, because its blood has an unusually high affinity for oxygen. It

LEFT The lemon shark, *Negaprion brevirostris*, is a favourite shark for laboratory research as, unlike many other sharks, it survives well in captivity. It has also been extensively studied in the wild by Sam Gruber and his colleagues at the Bimini Biological Field Station.

appears sluggish, but a neat physiological trick enables it to move remarkably quickly. It diverts oxygen-rich arterial blood to where it is needed and increases its gill surface by as much as 20% to draw more oxygen from the seawater.

The lemon shark feeds mainly at night on fish (including smaller sharks and sting rays), squid, crustaceans and even seabirds, and is found around docks, creeks, estuaries and shallow-water bays in the western Atlantic, off the coast of West Africa and in the eastern Pacific. During the day, it might be seen 'resting' on the shallow seabed, pumping water over its gills. An interesting development in the western Atlantic is the discovery of large aggregations of lemon sharks off Jupiter on the Florida coast from early January until late April. The aggregations appear to be linked to ambient sea temperature, the significant figure being 24 C (75 F). Most of the sharks are females, with males migrating repeatedly between Jupiter and sites further to the north, off Georgia and the Carolinas.

Little is known about courtship and mating, although females with mating scars are seen at Tiger Beach on the Little Bahama Bank, and males tagged off Florida have been tracked there too. This work and studies on the later stages of reproduction and pup development have been carried out by Sam Gruber and his team from the University of Miami. Centre of operations is the pupping site at a horseshoe-shaped atoll in the Bahamas called Bimini. Here, pregnant lemon sharks from the western Atlantic arrive between April and June to drop their pups. The pups, between five and seventeen in a litter and each about 60 cm (24 in) long, are born tail-first.

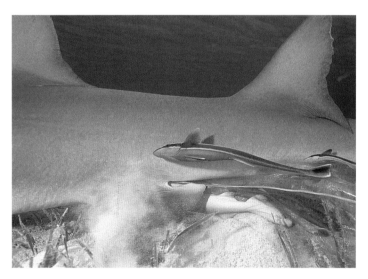

ABOVE A pregnant lemon shark gives birth in the relative safety of the Bimini lagoon in the Bahamas. Remoras dart in to eat the afterbirth.

As each one emerges, it lies momentarily on the sand, straining on the umbilical cord by which it is still attached to its mother. With a sudden jolt, the cord breaks and the pup is free and soon swimming for the safety of the mangroves that fringe the lagoon.

During their first year, the youngsters live in a section of mangrove about 400 m (1,312 ft) long by 40 m (130 ft) wide in water no more than 0.9 m (3 ft) deep. Here, they lie on the sand amongst the tangle of mangrove prop roots, taking occasional excursions into deep water. They feed on small fish, such as snappers and grunts, and invertebrates, such as shrimps and worms. Hidden amongst the mangroves, they are relatively safe from their main predators, larger sharks. As they grow older, they gradually enlarge their activity space, but there comes a time, at about two years old, when they leave the nursery areas completely and move to other sites within the lagoon. At each site only sharks of the same age and size associate together. They remain inside the lagoon until they are about seven or eight years old, when they head out towards the more open reef habitats, but they still do not travel far. They linger around the island for several years. However, at about eleven or twelve

LEFT Juvenile lemon sharks hide in the mangroves at the edge of the Bimini lagoon.

years old, the lemon sharks move away from Bimini entirely, making long migrations up and down the US coast, but returning during May, June and July to Little Bahama Bank, the Keys and Florida Bay where they are thought to meet for mating. The females have a two-year reproductive cycle. They mate, carry to term, and drop their pups in one year, and then rest for a year.

SANDBAR SHARK

The sandbar shark, *Carcharhinus plumbeus*, lives in tropical and subtropical waters in all the world's seas and oceans, including the Mediterranean Sea and the Adriatic Sea, where it used to startle gondoliers on the canals of Venice. It inhabits shallow coastal waters to a depth of 250 m (820 ft), and is frequently seen in estuaries. Spending much of its time close to the seabed, it feeds on bottom-dwelling crustaceans, molluscs and fish. It occasionally eats mid-water fish and squid, particularly in deeper water. Evidence of scavenging inshore comes with the remains of pork and beef refuse in sandbar stomachs.

Mature adults have a stocky body, and they grow remarkably slowly, reaching sexual maturity at a length of 1.7 m (5.5 ft), as late as 30 years old. They have a maximum size approaching 3 m (10 ft) – if they make it this far, for juvenile sandbars fall prey to many other shark species, including bull and great white sharks. Along the US Atlantic coast this has left a curious imbalance of the sexes: there are five females to every male.

Pregnant females enter the shallow-water nursery areas in bays and estuaries where they give birth, while the males move to deeper waters. The females reduce the risk of cannibalism by segregating the sexes. Delaware and Chesapeake bays, on the Atlantic coast of the USA, are traditional nursery sites. It mid-May, a female will ride in on a salt-water 'wedge' as the tide rises and drop up to 14 pups, each 50 cm (1.5 ft) long. She leaves the area while her newborn pups remain. They feed on small

The sandbar shark, *Carcharinus plumbeus*, is a common species seen in aquariums all over the world. These individuals are at the Maui Ocean Center, Hawaii.

fish, crustaceans and molluscs. Young sharks trade a safe haven for a monotonous diet, although the safety is only relative, for adult bull sharks *Carcharhinus leucas*, blacktip sharks *Carcharhinus limbatus* and blacknose sharks *Carcharhinus acronotus* enter these waters where they eat small sharks.

In the fall, when the inshore waters cool, the young sharks over-winter in offshore sites, and in subsequent summers, juveniles about 1.2 m (2–4 ft) long seek out the same shallow bays and estuaries that they occupied as pups, abandoning them when seven to eight years old, having grown to a length of about 1.2 m (4 ft). Thereafter they occupy coastal waters, close to the shore but some distance away from the nursery areas. Immature sandbars tend to travel some way north in summer, the waters around Martha's Vineyard, Nantucket Island and Cape Cod representing the northern limit of the species in the western Atlantic. All the sharks here are immature, between 8 and 24 years old, and they stay in mixed schools, feeding on bony fish, crustaceans, skates, rays and dogfish, from July to September, when the water temperature is about 19–27°C (66–81°F). As they grow, they venture into deeper waters over the continental shelf. A large number of subadult male sandbars are found in the region of the Hydrographer Canyon, to the east of Cape Cod on the edge of the continental shelf. It is the furthest north congregations of these sharks are found. In the fall, all sandbars move offshore and head south, the western Atlantic population passing the winter months off Cape Hatteras in waters about

LEFT Silky sharks, *Carcharhinus falciformis*, like this individual, are often seen feeding on tight shoals of small fish, alongside other marine predators, such as dolphins and tuna, but if oceanic whitetips, *Carcharhinus longimanus*, should turn up, the silky sharks defer to them.

140 m (460 ft) deep. As they grow, some undertake more extensive migrations, including excursions into and out of the Gulf of Mexico.

The dusky shark, *Carcharhinus obscurus*, and silky shark, *Carcharhinus falciformis*, make similar journeys. The silky shark is named for the smoothness of its skin, resulting from its very small, flat dermal denticles. It is a tropical shark, growing to 3.5 m (11.5 ft) long, and is often found in schools feeding alongside tuna and seabirds. A school will sometimes congregate beneath a floating log or other large floating object, such as a large naval target, a buoy, or a stationary boat in deeper water.

REEF SHARKS

Shallower waters in the Indian and Pacific oceans are home to several species of requiem sharks that live on or close to coral reefs. Each species avoids competition with others by exploiting different parts of the reef. Grey reef sharks, *Carcharhinus amblyrhynchos*, frequent clearer, deeper waters down to 150 m (490 ft) on the seaward side of reefs, while blacktip reef sharks, *Carcharhinus melanopterus*, are found on turbid sandy flats no deeper than 15 m (50 ft), and whitetip reef sharks, *Triaenodon obesus*, live among the nooks and crannies of the coral reef itself.

The grey reef shark can appear alone or in groups numbering 100 or more individuals. When feeding, these groups sometimes rush up from the depths,

RIGHT The blacktip reef shark, *Carcharhinus melanopterus*, can swim in very shallow water where it eats reef fishes, crustaceans and the occasional octopus. It is a common species on coral reefs and is frequently seen in aquariums.

RIGHT The grey reef shark, *Carcharhinus amblyrhynchos*, has an especially well developed balance system in its ear, useful in the confusion of feeding frenzies.

pinning schools of mullet and other reef fishes against the reef wall. They may have been attracted by sounds and vibrations, for in tests grey reef sharks are the first to appear when low-frequency sounds, similar to those made by struggling fish, are played back on underwater loudspeakers. It might also explain why spear-fishermen sometimes find grey reef sharks dashing in from nowhere and snatching the prize from under their noses.

The grey reef shark is a particularly aggressive species with a threat display (see pp.22–23) used against rivals, particularly when competing for food, or defending itself against large intruders, such as tiger sharks. One was once seen to threaten a hammerhead shark much bigger than itself. It will also threaten people. Grey reef sharks are not always aggressive to others of their own kind. They sometimes form schools that swim aimlessly back and forth along the reef or stake out deep-water channels between reefs. Females spend the day in a small core area of their home range, ignoring any prey that might swim by. Some fish, such as rainbow runners, *Elagatis bipinnulata*, streamlined members of the jack family that average 0.6 m (2 ft) long – take advantage of the amnesty. They follow the sharks and rub their bodies against the sharks' rough skin in what look like attempts to dislodge parasites. The sharks seem to ignore the runners totally. At dusk the schools break up and the sharks scour the reef edge for food.

Whitetip reef sharks tend to form schools at mating time. Hundreds of male sharks swim back and forth across the reef searching for females. An entire procession can form behind a receptive female, each male trying to grab her pectoral fin prior to mating.

ABOVE The fins of the whitetip reef shark, *Triaenodon obesus*, are sufficiently flexible to enable it to pass through narrow gaps.

More usually, whitetip reef sharks are found during the day resting on the sand or hidden in underwater caves and crevices. Several sharks might share the same bolthole, but at dusk they go their separate ways. They hunt amongst the coral during the night, pushing and squirming into narrow crevices and holes in order to get at the prey, such as small fish and octopuses. Small, pointed cusped teeth help them pull their prey from holes. They might break apart corals in their frenzied hunt, taking fish that are sleeping amongst the coral heads. After a night's fishing, they return to the same caves to 'rest'. The whitetip reef shark is one of the smaller requiem sharks, rarely exceeding 1.8 m (6 ft) in length. It has a squarish head, obvious nasal flaps and a distinct white tip to the anterior dorsal fin and upper lobe of the tail.

By contrast, the black tips to its fins distinguish the blacktip reef shark. It is also relatively small with a maximum adult size of 1.8 m (6 ft), but it more than makes up for its size with a particularly aggressive attitude. It will go for the legs of somebody wading over the reef, take speared fish, attack any fisherman cleaning his catch, and enter water only a few inches deep in pursuit of prey. It travels alone or in groups, and is often seen moving along the reef edge or along continental coasts. It eats

ABOVE The silvertip shark, *Carcharhinus albimarginatus*, has distinctive white tips and margins to its fins. It patrols the drop-off into deep water where it takes advantage of congregations of fish that depend on nutrient-rich upwellings from the deep sea.

small fish, squid, octopus, and shrimps, catching them with the help of narrow, sharp serrated teeth. It has a penchant for young groupers *Epinephelus*, but the tables are turned when the groupers grow up – they then feed on the sharks!

Other reef sharks include the silvertip shark, *Carcharhinus albimarginatus*, from Indo-Pacific reefs, and the Caribbean reef shark, *Carcharhinus perezi*, from the Atlantic. Both reach a maximum size of about 3 m (10 ft). The silvertip can be recognized by the bronze sheen to its upper body and the white tips and margins to all its fins. It is more streamlined and torpedo-shaped than the whitetip reef shark, and typically patrols waters below a depth of 25 m (82 ft). It also enters lagoons and other shallow-water areas where it tends to be very aggressive and to bully other reef sharks. The Caribbean reef shark is one of the most common sharks encountered on reefs in the West Indies, Florida, the Bahamas and the Gulf of Mexico. It inhabits the shallow reef areas, where it has been trained to receive free handouts at shark-feeding venues, although on some occasions it actually bites the hand that feeds it.

HAMMERHEADS

Hammerhead sharks are instantly recognizable by their curious T-shaped heads. There are nine known species, and each has a head of a slightly different size and shape. At one extreme is the broad wing-shaped hammer of the winghead, *Eusphyra blochii*, while at the other is the shovel-shaped head of the bonnethead, *Sphyrna tiburo*. It was thought at one time that the evolutionary trend was for increasingly broad hammers, but DNA analysis of tissues from a selection of hammerhead species, conducted by Andrew Martin, then working at the US Smithsonian Tropical Institute in Panama, has revealed the opposite is true. The winghead, with a hammer-width

LEFT The bonnethead, *Sphyrna tiburo*, is about 1.5 m (almost 5 ft) long. It is not an overtly aggressive shark, and a school will get along together without fighting. Large males dominate.

RIGHT The great hammerhead, *Sphyrna mokarran*, sometimes uses the side of its broad head to pin down a stingray on the seabed and then bites chunks out of its 'wings' until it has eaten its catch.

equal to half its body length, is the most ancient species of living hammerhead, whereas the bonnethead, with the smallest hammer, is the species to have evolved most recently. Under some unknown influence heads have become smaller with time, and scientists believe it might have something to do with an evolutionary conflict between the two quite different functions of the hammer-shaped head. More recently, Professor Martin and his team, now at the University of Colorado at Boulder, has revealed that hammerheads evolved abruptly from a requiem shark similar to the modern spadenose shark, *Scoloiodon laticaudus*, about 20 million years ago, and that big hammerheads probably evolved into smaller hammerheads and the smaller hammerheads evolved independently twice.

Hammerheads have taller dorsal fins and smaller pectoral fins than their requiem ancestors and most other modern sharks, an adaptation to bottom feeding. The shape of the head, however, offsets the loss in fin surface area. The wings of the head act as hydrofoils, similar in shape and function to the bowplanes of modern submarines. In cross-section, they have a flat underside and curved topside like a wing. They increase lift as the shark moves through the water. There is also evidence that the trailing edge of each wing behaves like the flaps on an aircraft's wing, and that these flaps can be controlled by special tube-like muscles that form part of the shark's jaw mechanism, boosting manoeuvrability. With this configuration, the hammerhead can make extremely tight turns.

The wings also spread the senses of sight, smell and electric field detection across the width of the hammer, creating a greater stereo-scanning area and improving prey detection. The leading edge and front underside of the wings are covered with the ampullae of Lorenzini, the fluid-filled pits capable of picking up the weak electric fields associated with prey. At a distance of 25 cm (10 in), a hammerhead can detect electrical activity from the heart muscles of a stingray hidden on the seabed. The nostrils are also wide apart, enabling 'stereoscopic sniffing'. In some species, such as the scalloped hammerhead, *Sphyrna lewini*, the channels that lead to the nostrils are spread across the front of the hammer where they function as the olfactory equivalent of ear trumpets. The shark progresses by sweeping its head from side to side, like a person using a metal-detector. To cope with all this sensory information, hammerheads have relatively large brains for sharks, though these do not extend, as was once believed, into the wings of the hammer.

The eyes are widely separated at the very ends of the hammer, and it has long been questioned whether hammerheads have binocular vision, but now Michelle McComb and colleagues, from Florida Atlantic University and the University of Hawaii, have tested a variety of hammerheads in captivity. They attached sensors to the skin to pick up brain activity and shone beams of light at the sharks from different angles. They confirmed that hammerheads do, indeed, have anterior binocular vision and therefore see ahead and judge distances. What is more, the degree of overlap between the two eyes increases with head width. In sharks with conventional pointed heads, such as the lemon shark, the eyes overlap by just $10°$, whereas the scalloped hammerhead overlaps by $32°$, and the winghead by $48°$. By swinging the head from side to side, hammerheads are also able to see behind them, and the position of the eyes on the ends of the hammer means they can see $360°$ in the vertical plane, so they can see above and below them at all times. As well as increasing their ability to spot and capture prey, the all round vision greatly benefits smaller individuals that must watch out for predators.

The head and fins aside, all species of hammerhead sharks have the same basic body plan as requiem sharks. They all bear 'live' young, each of their embryos being attached to the uterine wall of its mother by a yolk-sac placenta. After a gestation period of about seven months, most species give birth to large numbers of offspring, ranging from sixteen 35 cm (14 in) long pups in the bonnethead to more than forty 45 cm (18 in) long in the scalloped hammerhead and forty 75 cm (30 in) long in the great hammerhead *Sphyrna mokarran*. The youngsters are born headfirst with the wings of the head soft and pliable so that they bend backwards at the moment of birth, making life a little more comfortable for mother and babies alike.

THE VARIETY OF HAMMERS

Divers say that they can recognize a great hammerhead long before its head comes into view simply by the way it moves - by swinging its head from side to side. The great hammerhead often preys on bottom-dwelling stingrays and guitarfish, but takes fish from all depths. As its name suggests, it is the largest species of hammerhead, with recorded specimens up to 6 m (20 ft) long. It is found in all temperate and tropical seas and although not generally aggressive, it is thought to be potentially dangerous to people.

The smaller smooth hammerhead, *Sphyrna zygaena*, has an almost global distribution, reaching British shores in the eastern Atlantic and Nova Scotia in the western Atlantic in summer. It is rarely seen in equatorial waters, being present only around Hawaii in the central Pacific. Characterized by a long, narrow hammer without a notch at the mid-point, the smooth hammerhead can grow up to 4 m (13 ft) long. It prefers shallow waters less than 20 m (65 ft) deep, and frequents rocky reefs where it feeds on a variety of fish, as well as lobsters, squid, stingrays and other shark species.

The bonnethead, with the smallest shovel-shaped hammer, grows up to 1.5 m (5 ft) long. It inhabits the eastern Pacific and western Atlantic, but the Pacific sharks have a broader head than those in the Atlantic. At certain times of the year bonnetheads of

RIGHT This juvenile smooth hammerhead, *Sphyrna zygaena*, was found in temperate waters off the coast of South Australia. Schools of youngsters up to 76 cm (30 in) long also appear along the outer shore of Long Island near New York each August.

RIGHT The great hammerhead is found in shallow shelf waters in all warm temperate and tropical seas, where it preys on bony fish, sharks and rays. Here a jack is the victim.

GOLDEN SHARKS

One population of smalleye hammerheads lives in the muddy waters of the Orinoco delta and is coloured yellow. This golden shark, or 'yellow chapeau' as it is called locally, is the only shark known to take on the colour of the food that it eats. It feeds not only on bright yellow shrimps, *Xiphopenaeus kroyeri*, that are rich in betacarotene,

one source of its skin pigment, but also on yellow catfish with yellow eggs. The shark takes on its golden hue only when young. Pups are born in Trinidad's Manzanilla Bay and adjacent Matura Bay, and are grey above and yellow below at first. When they reach adolescence at 53–69 cm (21–27 in) they turn bright metallic yellow. At full maturity, when 1.2 m (4 ft) long, the intense colour fades to yellow blotches. The reason for the colour is unknown, but one suggestion is that it is a form of camouflage, enabling the young sharks to blend in with the clay-coloured slit suspended in the water. Young hammerheads, like the young of most sharks, are vulnerable at this stage in their lives to predation, mainly from other species of sharks.

LEFT The murky waters of the Orinoco reach as far north as Trinidad. Here the skin of young smalleye hammerheads, *Sphyrna tudes*, matches the colour of the water, the pigments responsible being the same as those found in carrots.

the same size and presumably the same age and sex congregate at the surface, but nobody knows why. They also migrate, moving to warm waters in winter and cooler places in summer. Food tends to be from the shallow sea floor and consists mainly of shellfish, octopus and squid. This shark has small, sharp teeth at the front of the jaws for grabbing soft-bodied animals and large, broad teeth at the back of the lower jaw for crushing hard-bodied prey. It is credited with one attack on a person, but is generally thought to be a docile, if not timid, shark.

Another hammerhead with a maximum length of 1.5 m (5 ft) is the winghead, *Eusphyra blochii*. It is found along coasts and around islands in the Indian Ocean and the western Pacific. Rather stouter than the other hammerheads, it has the broadest hammer. The head of a 1.5 m (5 ft) long winghead is 0.75 m (2.5 ft) across, and the wings are long, narrow and swept backwards.

Two other 1.5 m (5 ft) long species are the scoophead *Sphyrna media* and smalleye hammerhead *Sphyrna tudes*. The scoophead lives in the shallows of the east Pacific, from California to Ecuador, as well as the southern Caribbean and the southwest Atlantic. The smalleye hammerhead is found in the shallow waters of the southwest Atlantic, but is also known from the western part of the Mediterranean Sea. The smallest hammerhead is the mallethead shark, *Sphyrna corona*, which grows no more than 0.9 m (3 ft) long and lives in shallow tropical waters in the eastern part of the Pacific Ocean, from southern Mexico to Colombia. It is also thought to venture into the Gulf of California. The whitefin hammerhead, *Sphyrna couardi*, measures up

RIGHT Juvenile scalloped hammerheads, *Sphyrna lewini*, in the shallow waters of Hawaii's Kaneohe Bay take on a suntan. The amount of melanin in the skin can double when exposed to the sun – a trait they share with people.

to 3 m (10 ft) long and is found in the southeast Atlantic. Little is known about the biology or behaviour of these four species.

The most commonly observed species is the scalloped hammerhead (or kidney-headed shark), *Sphyrna lewini*. It has a maximum length of about 4 m (13 ft), and is widespread in warm temperate and tropical waters with temperatures above 22˚C (72˚F). It appears mainly in coastal areas and offshore waters to a depth of 300 m (1,000 ft), where it feeds on bony fish and squid. During the day it is often seen in huge schools.

HAMMERHEAD BABIES

Kaneohe Bay, Oahu, is the largest body of semi-enclosed water in Hawaii, and it appears to be an important pupping site for scalloped hammerheads. Here, juvenile sharks have been seen by Kim Holland and his colleagues at the Hawaii Institute of Marine Biology to form daytime schools in the murky waters. The youngsters begin to appear in April after females move into the bay to give birth. The pups forage far and wide across the bay and fringing reefs at night, routing out reef fishes and crustaceans, including alpheid shrimps, *Alpheus mackayi*, They return to the more turbid areas of the bay by day, where they form into loose schools and move about relatively slowly and randomly just 1.5 m (5 ft) off the sea floor. This behaviour can be seen until the last of the pups arrives in October by which time as many as 10,000 pups will have been born. The schooling of the juveniles is thought to be anti-predator behaviour. When they are of sufficient size to survive in the open sea, the young sharks leave the bay.

In most species of sharks any form of parental investment in their young stops at birth, but the scalloped hammerhead in at least one part of the world appears to extend the period of parental responsibility. Schools of hammerheads swimming in an unusual formation have been seen in the Red Sea, the adult sharks forming a protective outer shield, while a tight pack of youngsters, each no more than 2 m (6.6 ft) long, swims at its centre.

HAMMERHEAD SCHOOLS

The dramatic underwater spectacle of huge schools of hammerheads has been observed daily in shallow water at seamounts in the Gulf of California, off the volcanic islands of the Galapagos Archipelago, over an undersea pinnacle near Cocos Island to the west of Costa Rica, and in deep water near the coral atoll of Sanganeb in the Red Sea. At each of these places, 200 or more scalloped hammerhead sharks swim aimlessly up and down at what appear to be daytime 'roosting' or 'refuging' sites where the sharks neither forage nor feed, but appear to be resting. They all head in the same direction and are spaced evenly in the water column, swimming back and forth along the drop-off to deep water.

The school is considered to be a true school rather than an aggregation. The sharks deliberately stay and swim together, and when the currents around the seamount change they do not follow the most comfortable route, but continue along their preset and relentless course. If they should swim through a shoal of prey fish, such as green jack *Caranx caballus*, it is ignored. Sharks at the front seem to determine the direction in which they are all heading.

BELOW An enormous school of scalloped hammerheads, *Sphyrna lewini*, congregates each day over an undersea mountain at Cocos Island, two to three days sailing from Costa Rica in the eastern Pacific.

In the Gulf of California the composition of the scalloped hammerhead schools is a ratio of 6:1 in favour of females of various sizes. Large individuals are able to secure a place for themselves at the centre of the group, while smaller ones remain on the periphery. The older a female becomes, the less tolerant she is of her neighbours, so the largest sharks are spaced out more than the others, the formation maintained by constant bickering.

Dominant females strike juniors with the underside of the jaws, so a hapless subordinate can be recognized by the white abrasions on its head. Occasionally, a large shark will shake its head and shift dramatically to one side, in a behaviour known as the 'shimmy dance', or it might swim upside-down, or 'corkscrew'. The corkscrew manoeuvre takes place in less than a second. The shark accelerates in a tight circle and twists its body through 360˚, light from the surface reflecting off the white belly. Sometimes the movement ends with the performer butting the shark underneath. This bullying tactic is the preserve of the larger, mature females, their aggression directed at smaller, immature females who escape to the fringes of the school, shaking their heads submissively as they go.

The reason for this schooling behaviour is not totally clear. It might be the way that hammerheads rest during the day. Even sharks have enemies, such as killer whales and larger sharks, so there is safety in numbers. The school might also have a sexual purpose: the only males present tend to be older, mature individuals, immature males usually being conspicuous by their absence. While the school swims, a male darts into its centre, seeks out a large and desirable female, and beats his tail to one side to propel his body sideways towards her, thus revealing his clasper. If the female is receptive, the two sharks swim out of the school and drop down to the seabed where they mate. The structure of the hammerhead school, with its female dominance hierarchy, could help male sharks locate the best partners with the minimum of effort.

Whatever its function, the school breaks up in the evening and the sharks go their separate ways to feed. They travel in twos and threes, heading out into deeper water for 20 km (12 miles) or more. The sharks show remarkable navigational skills, arriving unerringly at areas in the ocean where fish and squid are known to congregate. They do not swim close to the sea's surface, where they would be able to observe the position of the sun, moon or stars. Neither do they swim along the bottom, where they could follow the topography of the sea floor. Instead, they swim in mid-waters, making vertical excursions like blue sharks, and following a fixed course much like an automobile driving down a straight motorway. Whatever heading they adopt to seek out a source of food, they take the exact reverse heading home. The navigational cue is thought to be magnetic fields associated with the seabed, seamounts and volcanic islands.

The volcanic rocks on the seabed are magnetized, the minerals within them aligned with the position of the north and south magnetic poles when the molten rocks cooled. The pattern and strength of magnetization varies, although the general trend is north–south. Volcanoes that push up through the ocean floor are like giant magnets, and the rivulets of lava that spread out from them like the spokes of a wheel create magnetic ridges and valleys. Hammerheads (and maybe other sharks on migration) possibly follow these 'magnetic highways' on their daily migrations, returning at dawn and falling into line as they join the endless daily processions.

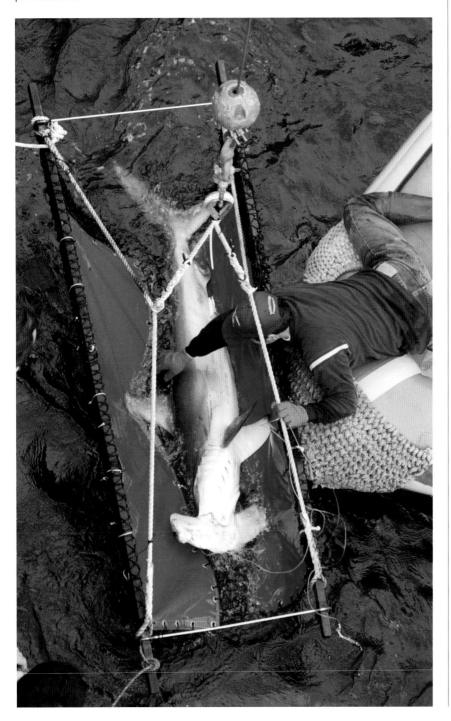

LEFT A scalloped hammerhead, caught by researchers working off Wolf Island in the Galapagos Islands, is fitted with an ultrasonic transmitter in a bid to find out whether these sharks prefer to congregate at one site or another. Results show that they do indeed, have a preference for one of two hotspots, which they visit daily. Researchers are now trying to find out why.

CHAPTER 5

Cats, dogs and a gentle giant

T HERE IS A MISCELLANY OF SHARKS without the typical fusiform shape of the streamlined hunters. Some of them swim close to or rest on the shallow sea floor, and have flattened bodies like skates and rays. In the family Pristiophoridae, for example, the sawsharks species *Pristiophorus* resemble the sawfishes *Pristis,* members of the ray group. The obvious differences are that sawsharks have shark-like pectoral fins rather than skate-like wings, and instead of the blade of the sawfish they have elongated, beak-like projections and two barbels that hang underneath. They feed on the bottom, where they are thought to plough into the soft seabed or rake through seaweed, disabling their prey by slashing it with the barbed snout. Baby sawsharks are born with their tooth-like projections lying flat against the snout, so they avoid damaging their mother's birth canal. They straighten out after birth.

OPPOSITE The whale shark is the world's largest living fish.

LEFT The common or longnose sawshark, *Pristiophorus cirratus*, grows up to 1.4 m (4 ft 6 in) long and is found in temperate waters on the southern fringes of Australia.

FLAT SHARKS

The 13 species of angelsharks, in the family Squatinidae, have a compressed body and extended pectoral and pelvic fins, but there the similarity with skates and rays ends. The pectoral fins are not fused at the front and are not used in propulsion. This is the function of the tail, which differs from the tails of most other sharks in having a longer lower lobe. Mature Atlantic angelsharks, *Squatina squatina*, can be up to 2.4 m (8 ft) long.

The skin on the upper surface of an angelshark's body is protected by spiky dermal denticles, while the underside has flattened scale-like denticles that enable the shark to glide over obstacles on the sea floor. It is able to rest flat against the bottom and pump water across its gills without having to swim, and has an enlarged spiracle behind each eye through which seawater can enter the pharynx rather than through the mouth. This avoids blocking up the system with debris and bottom sediments.

It uses these adaptations to catch a meal, and is a skilled exponent of the surprise attack. It lies on the bottom, hidden in sand or mud, and waits. It appears to rely less on the senses of smell, hearing and the ability to detect electricity, and more on vision. Lying dormant until something edible passes by, it suddenly rears up like some gigantic monster, opens its enormous mouth, and sucks in its victim. Flatfish, with which it shares the seabed, form the bulk of its food, but anything that triggers its lightening reaction can be sucked in accidentally including, on one occasion, a jar of mustard that dropped accidentally from a boat! It is active mainly at night and holds territorial rights over about 150 hectares (375 acres) of seabed. It travels from one ambush site to the next, clocking up 4 km (2.5 miles) each night. In the summer it tends to stay in water 30–100 m (98–328 ft) deep, while in winter it moves into deeper water, where mating is thought to occur.

RIGHT The Pacific angelshark or monkshark, *Squatina californica*, is found on the continental shelf along the Pacific coast of the Americas, from Alaska to southern Chile.

CAMOUFLAGED SHARKS

The wobbegongs that make up the family Orectolobidae blend in with their background even better than the angelsharks. They are bottom-dwellers, and are at home on the coral reefs of New Guinea and northern coasts of Australia. There are six species and each resembles a shaggy carpet lying motionless on the sea floor, camouflaged amongst coral and seaweed by an intricate pattern of spots, stripes and blotches on its back. The effect is enhanced further by a fringe of tree-like tassels, resembling fronds of seaweed, around its terminal mouth and jaws. Almost invisible, it waits for an octopus, crab or bottom-dwelling fish to chance by. Its prey is sucked into the vacuum caused by the sudden opening of its mouth. Sharp, needle-like teeth prevent the victim from escaping. Wobbegongs are not considered harmful to people, though if trodden upon accidentally they can give a nasty bite.

Another camouflage expert is the pyjama shark or striped catshark. *Poroderma africanum*, from the family Scyliorhinidae. It is a small longitudinally striped shark that is found on the South African coast. It is usually active at night, but it hunts in the day when food is plentiful, particularly in the squid-breeding season between October and December. At this time of the year various species of common squid in the genus *Loligo*, known locally as chokka, congregate in huge numbers at traditional breeding sites. The sluggish shark is no match for the high-speed squid, so it resorts to subterfuge. The squid deposit their eggs in communal sites, so the shark hides among the beds of eggs, its head buried but its tail curiously conspicuous. When a squid arrives to spawn, it dashes out and grabs it.

The zebra bullhead (or zebra hornshark), *Heterodontus zebra*, from the family Heterodontidae, has stripes that help it blend in with the colours of the coral reef in which it lives. Similarly, the brownbanded bamboo shark. *Chiloscyllium punctatum*

LEFT A fringe of fleshy barbels on the upper jaw of the spotted wobbegong, *Orectolobus maculatus*, completes its camouflage and enables it to blend in with its coral reef background.

RIGHT The Indonesian speckled carpetshark, *Hemiscyllium freycineti*, is one of the epaulette sharks. It is able to walk over the coral reef on its pectoral and ventral fins like a salamander.

RIGHT The Indonesian speckled carpetshark, *Hemiscyllium freycineti*, is one of the epaulette sharks. It is able to walk over the coral reef on its pectoral and ventral fins like a salamander.

– one of the long-tailed carpetsharks of the family Hemiscylliidae – has thick, wavy, brown bands around its body. The epaulette shark, *Hemiscyllium ocellatum*, another of the long-tailed carpetsharks, has many widely spaced black spots and one large black spot over each pectoral fin on either side of the body. The eel-like, necklace carpetshark, *Parascyllium variolatum*, one of the collared carpetsharks of the family Parascylliidae, has brown-and-white spots all over the body and a dark collar with white speckles in the area of the gills.

CATS, DOGS, HOUNDS, ZEBRAS AND NURSES

The common or lesser-spotted dogfish, *Scyliorhinus canicula*, has small brown spots, while its close relative the nursehound or greater-spotted dogfish, *Scyliorhinus stellaris*, has large brown ones. Although commonly referred to as 'dogfish', both species are really catsharks of the family Scyliorhinidae and they live in coastal waters in the northeast Atlantic. Of all the catsharks, the common dogfish is the most common shark people in Britain are likely to encounter. It is often exhibited in British aquariums and is sometimes found washed up on the shore. It also turns up at fish-and-chip shops served as 'rock salmon'.

In its natural environment, the common dogfish is an inhabitant of inshore waters where it feeds on molluscs, crustaceans and small fish. It has numerous small teeth and grows no longer than 1 m (3 ft). During mating the male curls his body around the female. She deposits about 20 eggs, each one protected in a translucent, rectangular egg case. The capsule has long, curly tendrils at each corner with which the female can anchor it amongst seaweed for the nine months that the embryo takes to develop inside. The pup is about 10 cm (4 in) long when it breaks free. It has brown stripes at first that later break up into spots.

LEFT The common or lesser spotted dogfish (sometimes called the small-spotted catshark), *Scyliorhinus canicula*, rests on the shallow sea floor by day and is active at night. It seizes prey by sucking water into its mouth along with the food.

Another shark that is sold as 'rock salmon' (or 'huss') is the piked (or spur) dogfish, *Squalus acanthias*. It is one of the dogfish sharks in the family Squalidae, and gets its common names from the spine in front of each dorsal fin. It lives in tropical, temperate, and sub-polar waters and where its plentiful it occurs in large schools that are segregated by size and sex. Packs of these sharks attack shoals of capelin, herring, and mackerel, and they will devour shrimps and other crustaceans, worms and jellyfish on the sea floor. They have even been seen to eat seaweed. The piked dogfish is an ocean traveller. In the Atlantic, specimens tagged off Newfoundland in July have been recaptured off Massachusetts in November, a straight-line distance of 1,500 km (900 miles). In the Pacific, an individual tagged off Washington State was caught off Japan about eight years later. Tagging studies have revealed it to be a very long-lived shark, with a maximum lifespan of over 100 years suggested.

It is an ovoviviparous species, the eggs retained inside the female's body in a tube known as the 'candle'. The litter of about ten embryos eventually breaks out of the candle but takes up to two years to develop, making the piked dogfish's gestation period one of the longest of all known vertebrates. It was once very common but its numbers have been reduced considerably by overfishing. Its slow rate of growth means that once populations are over-exploited they are slow to recover.

British sea anglers are quite likely to hook another long distance traveller, the tope *Galeorhinus galeus*. It is a relatively small shark in the houndshark family, Triakidae, that grows up to 2 m (6.6 ft) long. It is found on continental shelves and slopes in temperate waters all over the world, where it feeds on the bottom, taking fish, squid and octopus. Prey is grasped with pointed teeth that are deeply serrated on the rear-facing edge. The females are seasoned travellers. Tagging returns have shown that female tope in British and Irish waters make excursions to Spain, the Mediterranean, the Azores and as far south as the Canary Islands in the western Atlantic. They head south to give birth to their offspring; large females have litters of up to 50

ABOVE The soupfin or school shark (more often known as the tope), *Galeorhinus galeus*, gathers in schools and feeds on the seabed. This individual found off California might well turn up off the coast of British Columbia, 1600 km (1000 miles) away.

OPPOSITE The zebra shark, *Stegostoma fasciatum*, is a slow-swimming species. By day it rests on its pectoral fins on the shallow sea floor, facing into the current so that oxygen-rich water passes over its gills.

pups. Off the northwest Pacific coast of North America, where the tope is known as the soupfin shark, females also head south in summer to southern California to drop their pups. Tope are long-lived and slow to mature. Tagging studies off South Australia, where it is sometimes known as the school shark, have revealed that tope rival sandbars for slow growth. An individual thought to be about ten years old was tagged in 1951 and measured 1.35 m (4 ft 5 in) long, but when recaptured 35 years later it had grown only another 6.5 cm (6 in).

A shallow-water species with a similar basic shape to the nurse shark (below) is the closely related zebra shark, *Stegostoma fasciatum*, a species frequently seen on tropical coral reefs. It is in a family all of its own, the Stegostomatidae, and is recognized by the extremely long upper lobe to its tail. It has spots rather than stripes, its seemingly inappropriate common name referring to the striped pattern of the young. The stripes are lost as the sharks get older.

In the tropics, common species living in shallow, inshore waters are the nurse sharks in the family Ginglymostomatidae. Of the three living species, the nurse shark *Ginglymostoma cirratum* that lives along the southeast coast of the USA is the best studied. It is frequently seen in aquariums, and experiments in the 1960s showed that captive animals are capable of learning to press illuminated targets to receive a food reward. The tests showed that they could learn with almost 100% accuracy as fast as a mouse.

RIGHT A nurse shark, *Ginglymostoma cirratum*, forages for food in the Bahamas. Its common name may be derived from the audible slurping noise it makes when gulping and sucking up crustaceans and molluscs from the sea floor.

The nurse shark is a slow-swimming bottom-feeder recognized by the two barbels on its snout. Adults grow to about 3 m (10 ft) long. Groups of them are frequently seen resting on the sea floor. In June each year, one population in the western Atlantic heads for the Florida Keys to court and mate. For a period of about five weeks, the sharks thrash about in the shallows, as gangs of males chase after females, with each member of a group trying to seize the pectoral fin of a female in order to mate with her. A successful pairing lasts for about two minutes, after which the male heads for deep water to recuperate briefly before heading back to the shallows to try again.

GENTLE GIANT

The whale shark, *Rhincodon typus*, is the largest fish in the sea. Everything about it is big. It grows to over 12 m (40 ft) long, has a horizontal, slit-like mouth up to 1.5 m (5 ft) wide, and possesses a liver weighing up to a tonne. Its anterior dorsal fin can be up to 1.2 m (4 ft) tall, and its tail, with upper and lower lobes of similar size, can be enormous, up to 3 m (10 ft) from top to bottom.

The whale shark is not only big but also very conspicuous. Its markings – a brown-coloured skin with white spots and stripes – are easily recognized, and each individual has its own distinctive patterns. Three ridges run along each side of the body, and there is no tail notch as in most other sharks. The mouth is at the front of the broad head, rather than being underslung. The eyes are remarkably small for such a large animal, and the shark is able to swivel them back into the eye socket for protection. The skin on a whale shark's back is 10 cm (4 in) thick and very tough. It has a thick layer of gristly connective tissue underneath, and is covered with tiny overlapping 'teeth' (dermal denticles), each about 0.75 mm (0.002 in) long. The muscles below the skin can be tightened, making a structure as tough and impenetrable as a steel-braced truck tyre. Harpoons, buck-shot or rifle bullets just bounce off. It is invulnerable to just about anything but a ship.

Like the baleen whales, after which the species takes its common name, the whale shark is a filter feeder, straining out plankton, krill, squid and small fishes, such as anchovies and sardines from the seawater. The shark's mouth has thousands of tiny 2 mm (0.5 in) rasping teeth arranged in 12 rows, but these are not for filtering food. Instead, a mesh of fine gill rakers, consisting of numerous cartilage bars supporting spongy tissue derived from modified denticles is set on the gill arches. The filter they form has a mesh-size of about 25 mm (1/10th in).

Water enters the mouth, passes through the gill rakers and exits through the five large gill slits on either side of the body. It can be a passive process, with the flow of

BELOW The whale shark, *Rhincodon typus*, is instantly recognized by its spotted skin and the ridges running down its flanks. Why it should be so conspicuously patterned is a mystery.

GIANTS OF NINGALOO REEF

Whale sharks arrive at Ningaloo reef, on the west coast of Western Australia, close to the town of Exmouth, in late March and April each year. They appear precisely three weeks after all the corals on the reef have spawned at the same time and on the same night. The sharks do not feed on the spawn as such, for the contents of these tiny packages of sperm and eggs are too small for the whale shark to filter out. The spawn is food first for zooplankton, that thrives and is consumed by larger organisms, such as small fish, the larvae of mantis shrimps and swimming crabs, arrow-worms, comb-jellies, and a tropical species of krill, *Pseudeuphausia latifrons,* about 8 mm (1/4 in) long. It is for these organisms that the sharks congregate in large numbers.

Each southern autumn about 200 whale sharks, mostly 6–8 m (20–26 ft) long immature males, move in from deeper waters. Sometimes the sharks assemble in one area, twenty or thirty appearing together at dusk in a gargantuan feeding frenzy. They rush across the surface of the sea, their dorsal surfaces exposed and their mouths clearly visible as they filter organisms from the surface waters. Feeding can take place night or day, although it is thought the main bouts are at night. When the food runs out, the whales return to the depths of the Indian Ocean. Nobody knows where they go next.

RIGHT The Ningaloo whale sharks appear for just a few weeks after the corals have spawned.

water produced as the whale shark swims slowly forwards, or an active process when water is forced through the filtering system. The shark swims slowly but powerfully through surface waters at a steady 3–4 km/h (1.9–2.5 mph), but is able to suck in and filter seawater when stationary. When water is pumped through the slits, the covers flare out. It also can hang vertically in the water beneath a shoal of fish and, while gently moving up and down, suck in its prey. Sometimes, the mouth pushes above the surface, the water is drained out, and then the shark sinks down slowly with its mouth open, while water and fish pour in.

Whales sharks are oviparous. A 10.7 m (35 ft) long pregnant female, which had been harpooned by a Taiwanese fisherman and was dissected by marine biologists in 1995, contained 304 embryos, each between 40–65 cm (16–26 in) long, the largest number of embryos found in any shark. Most were in egg cases, each with a yolk sac. The largest had already hatched and were retained inside the mother's body. Recent DNA analysis on 29 embryos from that same shark, by Jennifer Schmidt, of the University of Illinois in Chicago, indicates that, even though the embryos were at different stages of development, they all had the same father. It seems female whale sharks are like sperm banks. They save up sperm after mating, the result being a queue of multiple litters, an insurance policy perhaps, against the slender chance of meeting another male in the vastness of the ocean.

Whale sharks are found in the warmer waters of the Atlantic, Pacific and Indian Oceans, but are absent from the Mediterranean. They make occasional forays into temperate waters, following warm currents such as the Gulf Stream, with claims of sightings off the Azores, Monterey Bay, and New York. More usually they are confined to seas with a temperature 20–26°C (68–79°F), in a band that encircles the globe between 30° north and 35° south. However, they have been recorded at depths in excess of 980 m (3,215 ft), where the water temperature can be 10°C (50°F) or colder. Whether they are long-distance travellers is becoming clearer, for their appearances at progressively more southerly sites off the east coast of Australia throughout the summer months indicate they probably are. In addition, Professor Schmidt's DNA studies of sharks from different parts of the world is showing very little genetic variation, indicating that whale sharks probably undertake extensive migrations with interbreeding between far-flung populations, maybe in different oceans. The longest migration recorded so far was an individual that travelled a distance of 13,000 km (8,078 miles) in 37 months from the Gulf of California, Mexico, to Tonga in the middle of the Pacific Ocean. Aside from reproduction, journeys probably take the sharks to areas where plankton blooms and marine invertebrates and fish spawn (see Giants of Ningaloo opposite). In the Caribbean, for example, many whale sharks turn up at Gladden Split on the Belize Barrier Reef where enormous aggregations of snappers spiral up to the surface to spawn. The whale sharks swoop in to scoop up eggs and sperm, but curiously ignore similar spawning events at 13 other known sites along the reef.

Measurements of whale sharks nowadays indicate an average length of about 9.8 m (32 ft), but in the past there have been claims of real giants. In 1905, a whale shark was impaled on the bows of the passenger liner *Armadale Castle* when it was steaming close to the equator. The captain estimated the shark to be about 17.4 m (57 ft) long. Off the coast of Honduras, 'Sapodilla Tom' was reputed to be a 20 m (66 ft) long monster that was seen regularly over a fifty year period, while in 1923 in Mexico's Bahia de Campeche, to the west of the Yucatan Penninsula, 'Big Ben' was said to be over 22.9 m (75 ft) long. The largest whale shark accurately measured was a specimen caught off Baba Island near Karachi, Pakistan, in 1949. The body length was recorded as being 12.65 m (41 ft 6 in) and its weight was estimated to be about 21.5 tonnes. The whale shark is classified in the order Orectolobiformes, along with the carpetsharks, wobbegongs, nurse sharks and zebra sharks, and is the only living representative of the family Rhincodontidae.

COOKIE-CUTTERS

Among the strangest of all sharks are the cookie-cutters. The two known species differ in size, but both have enormous, razor-sharp teeth. The one metre (3 ft) long largetooth cookie-cutter shark, *Isistius plutodus,* has a particularly impressive dental array, with the largest teeth for its body size of any known shark – even larger than those of its smaller relative, the 50 cm (20 in) cookie-cutter, *Isistius brasiliensis.* These small, odd-looking sharks use their formidable teeth in an unusual way. They live by day in the depths, down as far as 3.7 km (2 mi), where they feed on deep-sea shrimps and lanternfish. Each evening, they make a 3 km (2 mi) vertical migration to take them closer to the surface where they become opportunistic parasites, supplementing their diet by taking chunks out of larger animals. The technique they use is unique in the shark world.

Large creatures, such as whales, dolphins, marlin, swordfish and tuna are targeted. The tiny shark darts in and clamps on to its victim's body with its sucker-like mouth and huge razor-sharp teeth. Its tongue helps to create a vacuum for its suction grip. The forward motion of the temporary 'host' and the flow of water causes the shark to swivel, enabling it to rotate and twist off a plug of flesh about 5 cm (2 in) across, just like a cookie-cutter being used to cut out a disc of pastry. Victims can be spotted by the circular scars on their bodies, but the little sharks have not confined their attacks to animate objects. The rubber-covered sonar domes of US submarines have been attacked as well, mistaken for something more nutritious.

The cookie-cutter is found in all the world's warm seas. It has the curious habit of swallowing its own teeth, an adaptation no doubt to living in the depths where calcium is scarce. It has hook-like upper teeth in the upper jaw and razor-sharp, cutting teeth in the lower jaw. It swallows the entire front row of lower teeth in one go, the second row taking their place so the shark always has a full set with which to feed. Its scientific name has its root in Isis, the Egyptian goddess of light, on account of the photophores (light-producing organs) over its body. It is thought to be one of the most luminescent of all sharks. Its dull green glow appears to attract its inquisitive victims to within striking distance, but instead of a mouthful of juicy shark, they receive a nasty, golf-ball size bite in their side instead. The cookie-cutter will glow for up to three hours when taken out of water, its luminescence fading only when it is finally dead.

BELOW LEFT A Pacific spotted dolphin, *Stenella attenuata,* swimming off Hawaii bears a telltale circular scar, the recognizable bite from a cookie-cutter shark, *Isistius brasiliensis.*

BELOW The row of razor-sharp teeth of the cookie-cutter function just as its common name suggests – the teeth remove a disc of skin and flesh in the manner of a cook's pastry cutter.

DEEP-SEA CATS AND DOGS

Many of the dogfish sharks of the family Squalidae and catsharks of the family Scyliorhinidae live in the depths of the ocean so sightings are rare and little is known about their biology and behaviour. The false catshark, *Pseudotriakis microdon*, was first discovered in 1883, when a 3 m (10 ft) long specimen was washed ashore on Long Island, USA. It had a long, slender body, a long, low first dorsal fin, and small narrow pectoral fins. It looked like no other shark seen before, and very few have been seen since, although it is caught unintentionally off the coasts of Portugal, Iceland, the Cape Verde Islands in the Atlantic and in deep water in the Indian and Pacific Oceans. One was hooked as deep as 1,524 m (5,000 ft). The stomach contents of captured false catsharks include the usual mix of shark foods – other sharks, bony fish, squid and octopuses – but specimens hauled up from the deep Atlantic have contained such surprises as potatoes, a pear, plastic bags and soft-drinks cans.

Some sharks are found even deeper, in parts of the abyss where the pressure is enormous and the sea temperature can be as low as 5–6°C (41–43°F). One of the dogfish sharks, the 0.9 m (3 ft) long Portuguese shark, *Centroscymnus coelolepis*, is one of the deepest-dwelling of all known sharks, with a specimen caught in a fish trap reliably recorded at a depth of 2,718 m (8,917 ft). More usually, it is caught on long-lines, and a deep-sea fishery exists off the continental shelf of Portugal, from where the shark receives its name.

Another group of deep-sea dogfish sharks includes the gulper sharks of the genus *Centrophorus*. They are often photographed at baits set in the deep sea. They have wedge-shaped bodies and a maximum length of about 1.5 m (5 ft). Their skin has an unusual quality. Most sharks feel rough if stroked from tail to head, yet smooth if brushed the other way, but gulper sharks feel rough whichever way they are stroked.

In a family all of their own are the bramble or spiny sharks, the Echinorhinidae. Two species are recognized: the bramble shark *Echinorhinus brucus* and the prickly or prickle shark *Echinorhinus cookei*. They are known for the large and bramble-like dermal denticles that cover their bodies. They are rarely seen for they live at depths of 400–900 m (1,300–3,000 ft), but of those that have been caught or washed ashore, some have been nearly 3 m (10 ft) long.

Deep-sea roughsharks in the family Oxynotidae grow to a metre (3 ft) or more, have high, humped backs, stout bodies, a distinctly angular cross-section, rough skin and unusually large dorsal fins supported by sharp spines. They have a peculiar tooth arrangement, with a triangular patch of teeth on the roof of the mouth and slicing teeth in the lower jaw. Thick, soft lips surround the mouth. They cruise the deep-sea bed at depths of 30–500 m (100–1650 ft), where they feed on molluscs, crustaceans and echinoderms.

Many of the smaller dogfish sharks tend to roam the depths in packs, like underwater wolves. The green lanternshark, *Etmopterus virens*, has a brown

ABOVE The chocolate-brown-coloured Portuguese shark, *Centroscymnus coelolepis*, can grow to over 1 m (about 4 ft) long and lives deeper than any known shark.

body with a green iridescence, and grows to no more than 30 cm (12 in). Green lanternsharks feed on small luminescent fishes and deep-sea squid, and squid beaks found in their stomachs indicate that these small predators must overcome prey larger than themselves. The only way they could do this is to hunt in a group. It is thought that the luminescent organs carried on the flanks of this and many other species of small deep-sea dogfish sharks is connected with communication across a hunting school in the dark abyss, much like the white flashes on killer whales.

Some of these sharks are very small, but they travel great distances, not horizontally across the ocean, but vertically. The pygmy shark, *Euprotomicrus bispinatus*, which has small dorsal fins and light-producing organs on its belly, is one of these travellers. Its daily excursions take it from close to the surface, where it feeds at night, to depths of about 1,600 m (5,249 ft), where it passes the day. This means that this little shark, just 27 cm (10 in) long, has a vertical round trip of up to a kilometre each day, the equivalent of us running a marathon before breakfast and supper.

Among the smallest known sharks are two species discovered in 1985 off the Caribbean coast of Colombia: the cylindrical lanternshark, *Etmopterus carteri*, with

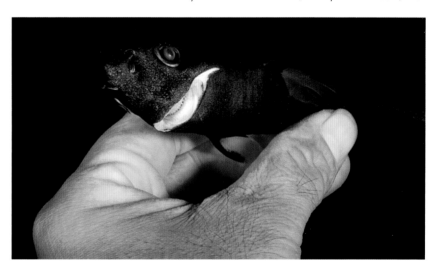

a maximum length of 17 cm (6.7 in) for mature males and 21.2 cm (8.4 in) for mature females, and the similarly sized dwarf lanternshark, *Etmopterus perryi*. Even smaller can be males of the spined pygmy or dwarf shark, *Squaliolus laticaudus*, known to the Japanese as *tsuranagakobitozama*, meaning 'the dwarf shark with the long face.' A mature male specimen caught in Batangas Bay on Luzon Island in the Philippines, in 1908, measured just 15 cm (5.9 in) long. Females are larger, with a maximum length of 25 cm (9.8 in). Like the pygmy shark, the dwarf shark joins the daily movement of predators and prey, spending the day close to the ocean floor, but ascending 200 m (656 ft) or more towards the surface to feed at night. It has luminescent organs on the underside of its body, and when observed from below against the glow of the surface, the shark is virtually invisible and therefore less vulnerable to other predators approaching from the depths.

CHAPTER 6
Sharks and people

A T ONE TIME SHARKS HAD a bad press, a reputation not helped by Stephen Spielberg's highly entertaining film based on Peter Benchley's book *Jaws*. The reality, however, is that sharks have more to fear from us than we have to fear from sharks. Nowadays, fear is being replaced by awe, respect and a real concern for creatures that have such an ancient lineage but are facing an uncertain future.

OPPOSITE Sharks and people can share the ocean without rancour, as long as the latter has more respect for the former.

SHARK ATTACKS

Sharks attack people and when they do so, these assaults can be life threatening or fatal. Attacks, however, are not at all frequent. There are more deaths from automobile accidents worldwide in one month than fatal shark attacks during recorded history, so you are more likely to be run over by a car on the way to the beach than be attacked by a shark in the water.

One of the first recorded shark attacks on a person was in 1580 and was observed by horrified sailors attempting to rescue a colleague who had fallen overboard on a voyage between Portugal and India. The man was thrown a rope but as the crew pulled him to the ship, a large shark appeared and tore him apart before they could haul him aboard. The record can be found in the International Shark Attack File (ISAF), a repository of information on shark attacks worldwide. It was set up originally in 1958 by the Shark Research Panel of the Smithsonian Institution and now resides at the Florida Museum of Natural History.

In a recent review of the files from 1999 to 2009, there were 64 recorded attacks each year on average, of which five were fatal. Taking into account parts of the world where statistics are not kept or attacks are suppressed because of the bad publicity, it is estimated there are no more than 70–100 shark attacks worldwide annually. In the USA, there is a 30 times greater chance of being struck by lightning than being attacked by a shark at the seaside, and

BELOW Sharks have been feared by sailors and shark attacks have been an inspiration for artists for centuries. Fuelled by persistent myths that sharks prefer human flesh, artists have had a field day.

SHARK ARM MURDER

The tiger shark, *Galeocerdo cuvier*, consumes just about anything it can find, and in 1935, its catholic eating habits placed one individual centre stage in a murder enquiry in Australia. The shark was caught alive in a fishing net and was given to the Coogee Aquarium in Sydney. It survived for a week, but during that time it regurgitated its stomach contents, which included a mutton-bird, *Puffinus* spp., and a human arm attached to a piece of rope. The arm was decorated with a distinctive tattoo, and was identified as belonging to James Smith, a member of the Sydney underworld who had been reported missing. Smith had been part of a gang of fraudsters who had fallen out over a bungled job. According to one of the gang who later committed suicide, Smith was eliminated, and his body stuffed into a metal box, except for one of his arms that was cut off, tied to a weight and thrown separately into the sea. The story would never have come to light if the captured tiger shark had not swallowed the arm.

bees, wasps and snakes account for a far greater number of fatalities. In fact, up to 150 people each year are killed by falling coconuts, according to George Burgess, Director of the ISAF. Nevertheless, when sharks strike, it is headline news. But does their attack behaviour reflect what the sharks themselves are doing or what we are doing?

Analysis of the long-term records since the mid-1800s by Leonard P. Shultz, an American fish biologist at the Smithsonian Institution, shows that half of all attacks occurred on people in the water between knee-deep and chin-deep. It also revealed that attacks occurred in all weathers, in clear or murky water, during the day or at night, in waters of any temperature, and in the open sea, on the coast, or in river mouths, and although sharks attack few people, they can do so at any time, and under any conditions. At one time rogue man-eaters and critical sea temperatures affecting shark behaviour were blamed, but there has been very little in the files to indicate that sharks deliberately target people. In fact, the data has indicated something quite different: that the frequency and pattern of shark attacks on humans has less to do with the behaviour of sharks and more to do with the behaviour of people in the water.

To check this out, a study by H. David Baldridge of the Mote Marine Laboratory was undertaken of human activity on Myrtle Beach, South Carolina. The results were illuminating: 17% of bathers were seen to congregate in knee-deep water. No less than 73% of swimmers were in water up to neck deep, which closely matches 78% of attacks taking place in this zone. Sea temperatures are generally over 20˚C (70˚F) when sharks attack, and the beach study found a simple explanation: people are reluctant to go swimming when the water temperature is less than 20˚C (70˚F). Below this temperature, there are fewer people in the water for a shark to attack, but as the sea temperature rises, the number of bathers increases, and, sure enough, the number of shark attacks multiplies too.

SHARK BITES

The Shark Attack File clearly indicates that any shark two metres or longer is potentially dangerous to people (apart from the two largest species, the huge whale and basking sharks, which are plankton-feeders that pose a threat only if they collide with a boat). There are four species in particular that dominate the headlines – the great white shark *Carcharodon carcharias*, the tiger shark *Galeocerdo cuvier*, bull shark *Carcharhinus leucas* and oceanic whitetip shark *Carcharhinus longimanus*.

Others implicated in attacks include the great hammerhead *Sphyrna mokarran*, shortfin mako *Isurus oxyrinchus*, porbeagle *Lamna nasus*, the species *Carcharias taurus*, known in the USA and elsewhere as the sand tiger shark, in Australia as the grey nurse shark, and in South Africa as the raggedtooth shark, blacktip shark *Carcharinus limbatus*, Galapagos shark *Carcharinus galapagensis*, Caribbean reef shark *Carcharinus perezi*, and grey reef shark *Carcharinus amblyrhynchos*. Between them they adopt any of four main unprovoked shark attack patterns.

'Hit-and-run' attacks frequently occur in the surf zone, where swimmers and surfers concentrate. Injuries tend to be minor, such as bites to arms and legs, and the attacks may be cases of mistaken identity. Poor visibility in the surf, coupled with a flash of jewellery or the white soles of feet may trick a shark into thinking a human is suitable prey. Having taken a bite, the shark realizes its mistake and leaves the area rapidly. A second type of attack involves mainly SCUBA divers who inadvertently enter a shark's personal space and receive a slash attack as a warning to keep clear. The third type, the 'bump-and-bite' attack is more dangerous. A shark may circle its victim and give it an investigating bump before the real attack. People in air or sea accidents are liable to this kind of attack. The fourth type is the 'sneak' attack. Approaching from below and behind, the shark attacks without any warning and it often results in severe and sometimes fatal injuries. It is the classic attack pattern of the ocean's top killers, such as the great white, tiger, bull and oceanic whitetip sharks.

People may also provoke or invite attacks. Grabbing a shark by the tail, even a docile one such as a nurse shark, *Ginglymostoma cirratum*, is not advised – although children on South Pacific islands do so as a game. Also some sharks, such as the Caribbean reef shark, *Carcharhinus perezi*, have been known to attack spear fishermen and grab their catch.

LEFT Shipwreck and air-disaster victims in mid-ocean are most likely to encounter the oceanic whitetip shark, *Carcharhinus longimanus*. Its sensory systems are alert to anything unusual and it approaches wreckage in the water without hesitation.

THE RED TRIANGLE

A large number of great white shark attacks on people take place in a triangular patch of the Pacific Ocean bounded by Monterey in the south, Point Reyes in the north, and the Farallon Islands in the west. It is known ominously as the 'Red Triangle', and it is like a magnet to great whites. They are not looking for people, but for seals – and elephant seals in particular.

By the early 1970s the intensively hunted northern elephant seal was on the brink of extinction, so a hunting ban

was imposed and its numbers increased. Conservationists were pleased – and so were the sharks. The sharks patrol the breeding rookeries and attack unwary seals in their traditional way – from below and behind, and with a rocky sea bed below so they blend in with their background. Attacks at the Farallon Islands tend to occur more frequently at high tide. With a premium on space, many of the elephant seals that haul out to breed on the islands are displaced when the tide is high and are then vulnerable to attack. There is also a peak of attacks in the fall, from September to December, when there are more young seals in the water. Unfortunately, divers or surfers near these seal rookeries are in 'attack-prone microsites', and are at risk.

LEFT These elephant seals resting on a beach on one of the South Farallon Islands bear the distinctive half-moon bite marks of a great white shark attack.

BELOW One of the first signs that a great white shark, *Carcharodon carcharias*, off California's Farallon Islands has attacked an elephant seal, *Mirounga angustivostris*, is a noisy flock of western gulls, *Larus occidentalis*, over the sea.

MISTAKEN IDENTITY

The motivation for an unprovoked shark attack is not always clear, but often as not the aggressor appears to have made a tragic error – the attack has been a simple case of mistaken identity, and the two shark species at the top of the shark attack league table are the ones making the most mistakes.

The great white shark is the number one people killer. It actually eats a variety of foods, including fish, sea turtles, skates and rays, and other sharks, but the more mature individuals are partial to seals and sea lions, and seen from below a person on a Malibu surfboard has an uncanny resemblance to a seal – not an ordinary seal, but one behaving in a strange way. Predators are predisposed to spotting aberrant behaviour, for it is an important part of their 'search image', establishing what is easy to catch and good to eat and where it is hiding. If the prey is sick or disabled, it is easier to overpower and devour without it fighting back.

From a great white shark's perspective a person on a surfboard silhouetted against the bright surface has the right image, so the shark approaches from below, races rapidly to the surface – like an express train, from eyewitness accounts – and attacks from behind, but by the time the shark has realized its mistake and the reality turns out to be a mouthful of foul-tasting neoprene and fibreglass, it is too late. The shark has already slammed into its target, but two out of every three great white attacks on people are not fatal. The majority survive an attack from one of the most powerful predators in the sea. Seals are the real targets, not people.

Similarly, tiger sharks – number two in the shark attack league tables – go for sea turtles. In Hawaii, where tiger sharks move into coastal waters looking for sea turtles that congregate near their egg-laying sites, body-boarders are at risk. A body-board plus body-boarder, seen from below, has a striking resemblance to the underside of a swimming sea turtle, so just swimming in a known sea-turtle area could be enough to invite an attack. If sharks were

BOTTOM LEFT The outline of a green sea turtle looks remarkably similar to a surfer on a short body-board. This makes the body-boarder a potential target for a tiger shark, *Galeocerdo cuvier*.

BELOW The silhouette of a surfer paddling on a surfboard looks remarkably similar to an aberrant seal, an attractive target for a great white shark, *Carcharodon carcharias*.

BOTTOM RIGHT A backlit California sealion, *Zalophus californianus*, is the kind of 'search image' that stimulates a great white shark to attack. The seal is unlikely to spot the shark approaching rapidly from below and behind.

ABOVE **A diver protected by a steel mesh suit hand-feeds an unpredictable group of blue sharks, *Prionace glauca*, as entertainment for an audience safely caged nearby.**

deliberately seeking out people, then there would be far more attacks. Hawaii's beaches are filled with bathers and surfers and tiger sharks frequent the surrounding seas, but the sharks rarely bite people, and those accidents that do occur are clear cases of mistaken identity.

OPEN-OCEAN OPPORTUNISTS

Open-ocean shark species live in what some researchers consider an aquatic desert, with meals few and far between. They are always alert for any opportunity to feed. Two sharks are likely to turn up for the feast – the oceanic whitetip and the blue shark.

Blue sharks arrive in a gang. They circle, sometimes for 15 minutes or more without incident, but then they tighten the circle, before moving in for the first 'test bite'. They are intensely curious, an adaptation to an open ocean life in which anything vaguely edible needs to be investigated. If the quarry is fit to eat, the sharks attack one after the other.

The oceanic whitetip is fearless. Unlike the blue, it swims directly to any object it considers prey and bumps it to assess its nutritional value before a fully-fledged attack. Oceanic whitetips were thought to have attended the tragedy of the USS *Indianapolis* during the Second World War. The warship was torpedoed by a Japanese submarine, and of the 1199 people who were thought to have left the stricken vessel just 316 survived. Survivors tell how they could look down into the clear water and see the sharks circling below before attacking without warning.

RIVER AND ESTUARY ATTACKS

Large rivers, such as the Amazon, Ganges, Mississippi, Congo, Zambezi and Limpopo, and lakes, such as Nicaragua in Latin America and Jamoer in New Guinea, often are patrolled by a species of shark that is able to spend time in fresh water. It is the bull shark, number three in the shark attack league table. Bull sharks have been seen many kilometres from the sea, and have been known to attack hippopotamuses and other river animals as well as people.

BELOW The bull shark, *Carcharinus leucas*, is one of the most dangerous of all sharks. It can eat anything at anytime, even in a river many kilometres from the sea.

It is considered by some authorities to be the most dangerous of all sharks, and many attacks attributed to great whites and tiger sharks could well have been the work of bull sharks. Such was the case at Matawan Creek on the New Jersey coast in 1916. Ironically, while hundreds of thousands of soldiers were being slaughtered in Europe, five shark attacks within ten days became front-page news worldwide. They were the most gruesome series of attacks recorded to date. Several sharks were caught, but attention focused on a 2.6 m (8 ft 6 in) long great white shark. In its stomach were the tragic remains of human victims – 7 kg (15 lb) of human flesh, a child's shinbone, and a rib bone. It was immediately hailed as the culprit, but whether the great white was responsible for the attacks or had simply scavenged the body parts is still debated today. Experts believe that a bull shark – the species more usually associated with brackish, estuary waters – was the shark responsible for the actual attacks.

THREATS TO SHARKS AND CONSERVATION

Sharks need friends. All over the world, sharks are big business, but obtaining reliable statistics is fraught with difficulties due, in the main, to illegal shark fishing. However, Shelley Clarke, of the Joint Institute for Marine and Atmospheric Research, University of Hawaii and National Research Institute of Far Seas Fisheries, Japan, and co-workers from around the world undertook a survey to assess global shark catch using a combination of trade records from commercial markets and genetic analysis to identify shark species present. It was the first fishery-independent assessment and it showed that the number of sharks caught and processed for the fin trade is 'three to four times higher than shark catch figures in the global database' compiled by the Food and Agriculture Organisation (FAO) of the United Nations. An estimate of the total number of sharks traded annually is between 26 and 73 million, with a mean of 38 million sharks.

Sharks are prime targets for sports anglers; shark-liver oils are added to cosmetics and health-care products because they are the nearest inexpensive oils to natural skin oils; shark skin is turned into luxury leathers for shoes, handbags and wallets; shark teeth are used as ornaments and in jewellery; shark cartilage can be a substitute for human skin to make artificial skin for burn victims; shark corneas have been used as successful substitutes for human corneas; a course of freeze-dried shark cartilage pills is claimed to arrest the growth of tumours; but by far the biggest and most lucrative market is dried fins for making into shark fin soup.

Shark fin soup is produced mainly in the Far East. It is a clear, glutinous broth that has been prepared from dried shark fins using traditional recipes for over 2,000 years. Once a rare delicacy, consumed only by Chinese aristocracy, it is today a gourmet food on sale in restaurants in Hong Kong, for example, for US$30-40 a bowl, a recent drop in prices linked to the world recession and the high price of oil for fishing boats. Even so, the market is reported to be growing at 5% each year, especially on

ABOVE Row upon row of shark fins dry in the sun at Kesennuma, a centre for shark fins in Japan. Included here are the caudal (tail) fins of blue sharks, *Prionace glauca*.

the Chinese mainland, with over half of retail sales to people hosting a celebration or other such gathering, according to a World Wide Fund for Nature survey. Such is the demand for fins and the remuneration so great, unscrupulous fishermen catch sharks, cut off their fins and throw their living bodies back into the sea, where they cannot move or swim and either starve to death or drown. This barbaric practise is known as 'finning' and thankfully it is now illegal in certain parts of the world, including in US waters, but it is still widespread and generally unregulated. It is also sobering to find that catching sharks for the fin trade is not confined to developing nations. A third of shark fins imported by Hong Kong comes from Europe.

Ironically, Mother Nature is about to get her own back. The traditional way in which shark fin soup is prepared means that the water content is reduced when the fins are dried and any impurities are concentrated. Nowadays, shark fins are laced with marine pollutants, such as mercury, and tests conducted at the University of Hong Kong discovered that the fins they analysed contained 5.84 parts per million (ppm) of mercury, compared to a maximum permitted level of 0.5 ppm. In Texas, similar tests with fresh sharks have revealed mercury levels up to 15 ppm, together with various other heavy metals, such as lead, even before the fins were dried.

Shark fin soup is said to be an aphrodisiac, and many people consume it specifically for this supposed property, yet the Hong Kong researchers also revealed that, because of the high mercury content, eating shark fin soup could render men sterile – the opposite of the intended effect.

OVERFISHING

With all this commercial interest, the temptation is for fishermen to catch every shark they can find, no matter what the biological or economic consequences. Shark fisheries, like the whaling industry before them, tend to follow a simple and predictable cycle of boom-and-bust. The problem is that sharks are slow to make more sharks, and if the breeding population is removed wholesale, the shark population and its fishery collapses.

The sandbar shark, which was caught commercially in the northwest Atlantic, illustrates this predicament. The species takes up to 30 years to mature; sexually mature females have offspring every two to three years and they have no more than 14 youngsters at a time, many of which fall prey to bull and tiger sharks before their first birthday. With a slow turnover like this, the population is slow to recover from heavy exploitation. In the sandbar's case, the problem is made worse because it passes from one local fishery to the next on its long-distance migrations in and out of the Atlantic Ocean and the Gulf of Mexico. The travelling population is diminished not once, but several times.

However, sharks that do not travel far are not excluded from suffering huge losses. For a shark population that remains in a small geographical area, commercial fishing could be nothing short of devastating and some populations fail to recover at all. A classic example was the rise and fall of two basking shark fisheries on the west coast of Ireland. The first was between 1770 and 1830 at Sunfish Bank (sunfish is the name given to the basking shark on account of its habit of basking in the sun with its back above the surface), about 30–40 km (19–25 miles) off the coast of Galway and Mayo near the edge of the continental shelf. The season was short, lasting only during April and May, but at least 1,000 sharks were taken each year at the peak of the fishery. In the early 1830s, the sharks became scarce. Despite continued high prices for basking shark oil, the fishery collapsed and failed to recover.

A hundred years later, the west coast population of sharks was sufficient to support another fishery, this time working from the land at Achill Island. At the end of April each year, hardy Irish fishermen would go after the muldoans, as they were known, stretching an entangling net across Achill's Bay of Keem and taking up to 30 sharks a day until the end of the season in August. Up to 1,800 sharks were taken each year between 1951 and 1955, but from 1956 the catch declined significantly. From 1956 to 1960 the average annual catch was 489 sharks, from 1961 to 1965 it dropped to 107, and then 50–60 per year until the fishery ended in 1975. A new fishery off Waterford in southeast Ireland in the same year, when 350 sharks were taken per year, confirmed that basking shark products were still in demand. At Achill Island, the sharks just were not there. It has been estimated since that the shark population declined by over 80% in less than ten years. Today, 35 years after the fishing stopped, sharks are beginning to return. During the summer of 2010 record numbers of basking sharks were sighted and tagged by the Irish Basking Shark Study Group north of Achill Island at Dunaff and Malin Head, so the population might well be recovering.

ABOVE Juvenile scalloped hammerheads, *Sphyrna lewini*, are caught in the Sea of Cortez for their fins and meat. Scientists report a significant reduction in the numbers of sharks seen in hammerhead schools, perhaps the first signs of over fishing.

RIGHT A scalloped hammerhead, *Sphyrna lewini*, caught by a sports angler, is being taken back to port for a Miami fishing tournament. Increasingly, anglers are encouraged to tag their catches and return them to the sea.

The reality of this 'boom-and-bust' effect, however, came home to shark researchers at the University of Miami who were studying the lemon sharks in Florida Bay. They netted sharks, tagged them and released them back to the sea. In 1986 the programme netted more than 150 lemon sharks, but in 1988 the catch had dropped to 42. In 1989 only 14 sharks were netted, and the following year the programme had to be terminated. Lemon sharks on migration, like the sandbar sharks, were suffering huge losses from commercial fisheries, but what is the impact of a population crash on undersea communities?

The marine environment has evolved over millions of years to maintain a dynamic equilibrium, and each component is important in the grand plan. Remove one element and order breaks down, the system thrown out of balance. Sharks are often the top predators in an ecosystem, and we know little about what happens when such an important component is removed. What are the knock-on effects further down the food chain? Sharks cull the sick, old and injured and scavenge on the dead, so their disappearance could have untold effects on not only local marine communities but also other commercial fisheries. On the Atlantic coast of southeast USA, for example, collapsing populations of mako and hammerhead sharks allowed their natural prey – the cownose ray *Rhinoptera bonasus* – to increase greatly in numbers. The rays feed on shellfish, and during 2004 the local scallop fisheries declined dramatically.

A CHANGE OF HEART

Such has been the concern worldwide for the fate of one species – the great white shark – that it has been singled out for individual attention, accompanied by an extraordinary U-turn in public attitude. At one time the great white was generally maligned, but this hostility has been replaced with concern by a more informed and an increasingly vociferous breed of shark-protectors.

Great whites, particularly the large breeding females, have been the target of a lucrative sports angling and trophy market, but in the 1990s an obvious decline in populations and the new, enlightened attitude culminated in the introduction of legislation in several countries. South Africa was one of the first to protect its great white sharks. Here it is breaking the law to hook a great white within 200 nautical miles of the coast, and it has been so since April 1991. Tasmania, Namibia and the Maldives followed South Africa's example, and then on 24 September 1999 Malta became the first European country to ban the fishing of great whites.

Two years previously, there was a flurry of political activity elsewhere in the world. In April 1997, the US National Marine Fisheries Service finalized a rule that included a complete ban on commercial fishing of great whites and confined recreational fishing to a tag-and-release program along the Gulf and Atlantic coasts of the USA. Killing great white sharks in Californian coastal waters was made illegal on 2 August, when Governor Pete Wilson signed a bill that afforded the species permanent protection indefinitely.

Across the other side of the world, from 17 December 1997 the great white shark was officially protected in Australian Commonwealth waters. It was made

SHARK SPECIALIST GROUP

ABOVE This shark is the unintended victim of another fishery. It is just one of an estimated 12 million-plus sharks that end up each year as bycatch from commercial fisheries.

In 1991, the International Union for Conservation of Nature (IUCN), established the Shark Specialist Group, part of the Species Survival Commission, set up to examine the conservation issues related to sharks, rays and chimaeras – the cartilaginous fishes. In 2009, the group reported on the status of selected shark species, regionally and globally, including a list of threats to their survival. They concluded that of all species of sharks and rays, 30% are threatened with extinction. Listed by the IUCN as 'endangered', meaning they are facing a high risk of extinction in the wild, for example, are two species of hammerhead, the scalloped hammerhead, *Sphyrna lewini* and the great or squat-headed hammerhead, *Sphyrna mokarran*. These along with other hammerheads, are often the victims of 'finning' for they have high quality fins but low quality meat. Other 'endangered' sharks include several species of angelshark, *Squatina* spp., and the Borneo shark, *Carcharhinus borneensis*, first identified in 1859, but the last record of it was in 1937. However, in 2007, researchers from the Borneo Marine Research Institute 're-discovered' the shark during a fisheries survey along the coasts of Sabah and Sarawak.

Sharks considered 'vulnerable', which means they are at high risk of endangerment in the wild, include the smooth hammerhead *Sphyrna zygaena*, great white shark *Carcharodon carcharias*, porbeagle *Lamna nasus*, basking shark *Cetorhinus maximus*, sand tigers *Carcharias* spp., and *Odontaspis* spp., dusky shark *Carcharhinus obscurus*, sandbar shark *Carcharhinus plumbeus*, night shark *Carcharhinus signatus*, oceanic whitetip shark *Carcharhinus longimanus*, smoothtooth blacktip shark *Carcharhinus leiodon*, tope *Galeorhinus galeus*, piked dogfish *Squalus acanthias*, whale shark *Rhincodon typus*, and the common, bigeye and pelagic threshers *Alopias* spp., all with populations still in decline.

Among the rarest of sharks are the Pondicherry shark, *Carcharhinus hemiodon*, known from 20 specimens in museums but only one found in a market in Karachi, Pakistan in 1974, and the Ganges river shark, *Glyphis gangeticus*, known from just three museum specimens that were hauled out of the Ganges-Hooghly river system about 100 years ago. Then, in 1996, a 2.8 m (9 ft) long female was caught, confirming the species was not yet extinct. Both are listed as 'critically endangered' in the IUCN Red List with the population declining, which means they are facing an extremely high risk of extinction in the wild in the immediate future. Similarly, the New Guinea river shark, *Glyphis garricki*, and the Irrawaddy river shark, *Glyphis siamensis*, are listed as 'critically endangered', as well as the daggernose shark, *Isogomphodon oxyrhynchus*, from the northern coasts of South America, and the sawback angelshark, *Squatina aculeata*, from coasts bordering the Iberian Peninsula, the smoothback angel shark, *Squatina oculata*, and the once common angel shark, *Squatina squatina*, both from the northeast Atlantic and Mediterranean.

The rot is also creeping into the deep sea. As populations of near-shore species are fished out, commercial fisheries are turning more to deep-water sharks, and already several species are threatened. The gulper shark, *Centrophorus granulosus*, has been listed as 'vulnerable' due to heavy deepwater fisheries in the northeast Atlantic, and Harrison's deep-sea dogfish, *Centrophorus harrissoni*, found off southeast Australia, is considered 'critically endangered'. One problem is that many sharks are threatened not necessarily from directed fisheries, but as a bycatch from other fisheries, and this hazard is badly documented. Some estimates indicate that more than 12 million sharks and rays per year are being taken as bycatch, 6.5 million of these being blue sharks. After decades of being a low priority, with little investment in research, monitoring or management, the current growing international concern has brought the shark centre stage; the question in whether this flurry of activity is too little, too late.

LEFT Humankind and the whale shark, *Rhincodon typus*, come face to face at Ningaloo Reef in Western Australia. The future of whale sharks and all of the other sharks in the ocean is very firmly in our hands.

RIGHT A group of amateur divers experiences the thrill of being close to sharks as an experienced shark handler feeds Caribbean reef sharks, *Carcharhinus perezi*, in the Bahamas.

illegal for people to take or kill these sharks, already considered 'vulnerable' under the Endangered Species Act, except for researchers with a scientific permit. Shark-fishing boats have now turned to shark-cage diving, and adventurous tourists who want to come face to face with one of the ocean's most spectacular predators have replaced sports anglers. And, in 2004, Australia and Madagascar successfully listed the great white shark on Appendix II of the Convention on International Trade on Endangered Species of Fauna and Flora (CITES), which restricts trade.

The plight of other sharks is beginning to be noticed. The sand tiger (grey nurse) shark in the USA and Australia, the whale shark in the Maldives, Philippines, the state of Western Australia and along the Atlantic and Gulf coasts of the USA, the shortfin mako in Canada, and the basking shark in USA, the Mediterranean Sea and in British waters are all now legally protected. Maybe a few sharks in some parts of the world have a future after all.

Glossary

AMMONITES Ancient group of animals, related to squid and cuttlefish, that lived in spiral shells like the modern pearly nautilus. They are now all extinct.

ANAL FIN Unpaired fin located posterior to the anus, which is present on the underside of most, but not all, sharks.

BIOLUMINESCENCE Living light – the production of light by living organisms without heat.

BIVALVES Mollusc with no head and with soft parts enclosed between two oval or elongated calcareous shells or valves.

BLUBBER Thick layer of fatty tissue under the skin of marine mammals that insulates them against the cold.

BONY FISHES Fish with skeletons made of bone.

CARTILAGINOUS FISHES Fish with skeletons made of cartilage, the same flexible material that forms your nose.

CLASPERS A pair of cylindrical extensions of the male shark's pelvic fin, used to transfer sperm to the female.

CLOACA A single aperture on the ventral (lower) side of a shark where the gut, and the urinary and reproductive systems open.

COPEPODS A large class of mostly marine crustaceans, including many external parasites that live on sharks and other fish.

CRUSTACEANS Hard-bodied animals without backbones, including crabs, lobsters, shrimps, woodlice, copepods, and barnacles.

DORSAL FIN The large triangular fin on a shark's back. Some sharks have a large anterior and a small posterior dorsal fin, while others have just a single dorsal fin.

EMBRYO Young animal that develops from a fertilized egg and is contained inside an egg case or within its mother's body.

GASTROPODS Molluscs with a head, an unsegmented body and a single, broad flat 'foot'. The group includes slugs and snails.

GEOMAGNETIC FIELD The field of magnetism surrounding the Earth that causes a compass needle to align north–south, no matter where you are on the Earth's surface.

HYDRODYNAMIC Describes an animal that is able to move through the relatively dense medium of water with considerable ease.

IMMUNOGLOBULIN Complex protein produced as a defence substance in response to a foreign body, such as a bacterium or virus, invading the body. It kills the invaders or renders them harmless. Also known as an antibody.

ISOPODS Flattened crustaceans, such as slaters and woodlice, which live in a diversity of habitats, from the deep sea to gardens. They also include 'fish lice', external parasites that live on sharks and other fishes.

JAWLESS FISHES Fish-like animals with backbones, no jaws and sucker-like mouths. They were among the first vertebrates to evolve in the Ordovician (500–430 million years ago) and developed into heavily armoured fishes. Most are now extinct, the survivors being lampreys and hagfish.

LONG-LINE FISHING Fishing line with hundreds of baited hooks that may stretch for as much as a kilometre down into the deep sea.

MOLLUSCS Animals without backbones that possess a mantle that secretes shell material. Includes a diverse group of animals from snails to squid, and from clams to pearly nautilus.

NICTITATING MEMBRANE Lid-like protective membrane that can be drawn across the eye.

PARASITE A small animal that lives on and obtains food from a bigger animal, in a relationship that is of no benefit to the host and may actually harm it.

PECTORAL FINS Pair of fins positioned just behind the gills that resemble aircraft wings in many species of sharks.

PELVIC FINS Pair of fins positioned on the underside of a shark, between the pectoral fins and the anal fin (if present).

PHEROMONE A chemical substance produced and released into the environment by an animal, which affects the behaviour or body of another animal.

STOMACH EVERSION The ability of animals, such as sharks, to push the stomach out of the mouth in order to get rid of hard, indigestible matter, such as the shells of sea snails or the carapaces ('shells') of sea turtles.

TAPEWORM Flat, worm-like internal parasite that usually lives in the gut of its host, but which lacks a gut itself.

UTERUS (WOMB) PLURAL UTERI One of a pair of muscular expansions of the female shark's reproductive system that contains the developing embryos. Some sharks have a pair of functional uteri and others have just one.

YOLK SAC A sac containing yolk which nourishes the developing embryo.

ZOOPLANKTON Small aquatic animals, consisting of small crustaceans and the floating larvae of larger organisms, which feed on the minute plants (phytoplankton) floating at the surface of the sea.

Further information

FURTHER READING

A Field Guide to the Sharks of British Coastal Waters, Philip Vas. Field Studies Council, Shrewsbury, England, 1991.

Discovering Sharks, edited by Sam Gruber. American Littoral Society, New Jersey, 1990.

Great White Sharks: The Biology of Carcharodon carcharias, edited by A. Peter Klimley and David Ainley. Academic Press, San Diego, 1996.

Sharks, Doug Perrine. Colin Baxter Photography, Grantown-on-Spey, Scotland, 1995.

Sharks: An illustrated encyclopedic survey by international experts, consultant editor John Stevens. Merehurst Press, London, 1987.

Sharks in Question: The Smithsonian Answer Book, Victor G. Springer and Joy P. Gold. Smithsonian Institution Press, Washington, D.C. 1989.

Sharks of the World, Leonard Compagno, Marc Dando and Sarah Fowler. Princeton Field Guides, Princeton University Press, New Jersey, 2005.

Sharks: Silent Hunters of the Deep. Reader's Digest, Sydney Hills, Australia, 1986.

Sharks! The Mysterious Killers, Downs Matthews. Discovery Channel Books, Park Lane Press, New Jersey, 1996.

The Little Guides: Sharks, consultant editor Leighton Taylor. Time Life Books, London, 2000.

The Sharks of North American Waters, José I. Castro. Texas A&M University Press, College Station, 1983.

INTERNET RESOURCES

NB. Web addresses are subject to change.

Bimini Research Station http://www6.miami.edu/sharklab

Florida Museum of Natural History http://www.flmnh.ufl.edu/fish/sharks/sharks.htm

International Shark Attack File http://www.flmnh.ufl.edu/fusg/Sharks/ISAF/ISAF.htm

IUCN Shark Specialist Group http://www.iucn.org

Mote Marine Laboratory http://www.mote.org

Pacific Shark Research Center http://psrc.mlml.calstate.edu

ReefQuest Centre for Shark Research http://www.elasmo-research.org/

Shark Research Institute http://www.sharks.org

Tagging of Pacific Predators http://www.topp.org

The American Elasmobranch Society http://elasmo.org

The Shark Trust http://www.sharktrust.org

White Shark Trust http://www.whitesharktrust.org/pages/index.html

Index

Credits

PICTURE CREDITS

p.4 © Gerard Lacz/FLPA; p.6 top © Jeff Rotman/Seapics.com, middle, bottom © Jeff Rotman/BBC Natural History Unit; p.7 Mike Eaton/NHM; p.8 © Nigel Marsh/Seapics.com; p.9 © Tom Campbell; p.10 top © Doug Perrine/Seapics.com, bottom left © Tom Campbell, bottom right © Andrea Marshall; p.11 © Andrea Marshall; pp.12-15 Mike Eaton/© NHM; p.16 © Mark Conlin/Seapics.com; p.17 © James D Watt/Seapics.com; p.18 Mike Eaton/© NHM; p.19 © Doug Perrine/Seapics.com; p.20 © Richard Hermann/Seapics.com; p.21 © James D Watt/Seapics.com; p.22 Mike Eaton/© NHM; p.24 left Niall Benvie/BBC Natural History Unit, right © Bob Cranston/Seapics.com; p.25 top left © Marta Nammack, top right © Doug Perrine/Seapics.com, bottom right © Tom Campbell; p.26 top, bottom © Jeff C. Carrier/Seapics.com; p.30 © Franco Banfi/Photolibrary; p.32 Philip Rye/© NHM; p.38 © David Shen/Seapics.com; p.39 © 2007 Getty Images; p.41 © Bob Cranston/Seapics.com; p.42 © Mark Conlin/Seapics.com; pp.43-44 © George Benz/Seapics.com; p.46 © Bruce Rasner/Seapics.com; p.48 © Reinhard Dirscherl/Photolibrary; p.49 Mike Eaton/© NHM; p.50 © Howard Hall/Seapics.com; p.51 © Robert Yin/Seapics.com; p.53 © Tom Campbell; p.54 top © Amos Nachoum/Seapics.com, middle & bottom © C & M Fallows/Seapics.com; p.57 © Gregory Skomal; p.59 © Dan Burton/Seapics.com; p.60 © Tom Campbell; p.62 © Dan Burton/Seapics.com; p.64 © Jeff Rotman/Nature Picture Library; p.65 © Doug Perrine/Seapics.com; p.66 © Leo Dickinson/BBC Natural History Unit; p.67 © Tim Clark/Seapics.com; p.68 © Doug Perrine/Seapics.com; p.70 © Masa Ushioda/Seapics.com; p.71 © Marty Snyderman/Seapics.com; p.72 © Tom Campbell; p.73 © Doug Perrine/Seapics.com; pp.74-75 © Doug Perrine/Seapics.com; p.76 © Doug Perrine/Seapics.com; p.77 © Tom Campbell; p.78 top © Masa Ushioda/Seapics.com, bottom © Steve Drogin/Seapics.com; p.79 © Tom Campbell; p.80 © Doc White/BBC Natural History Unit; p.81 © Doug Perrine/Seapics.com; p.82 © Gary Adkison/Seapics.com; p.84 top © Rudie Kuiter/Seapics.com, bottom © Gary Adkison/Seapics.com; p.85 © Doug Perrine/Seapics.com; p.86 © Masa Ushioda/Seapics.com; p.87 © Avi Klapfer/BBC Natural History Unit; p.89 © Pete Oxford/Minden Pictures/FLPA; p.90 © James W Kay/Photolibrary; p.91 © Marty Snyderman/Seapics.com; pp.92-94 © Tom Campbell; p.95 © Alan James/BBC Natural History Unit; p.96 © Mick McMurray/Seapics.com; p.97 Doug Perrine/Seapics.com; p.98 © Tom Campbell; p.99 © James D Watt/Seapics.com; p.100 © Tom Campbell; p.102 left © David Fleetham/Seapics.com. right © Gwen Lowe/Seapics.com; p.103 © John Morrissey/Seapics.com; p.104 top © Rudie Kuiter.Seapics.com, bottom © Masa Ushioda/Seapics.com; p.106 © David Fleetham/Nature Picture Library; p.107 *Die Fische, Brehms Tierleben*, edn. 3, A.E. Brehm. Leipzig, 1892; p.109 © Masa Ushioda/Seapics.com; p.110 top& bottom © Kenneth J. Goldman, Virginia Institute of Marine Science; p.111 top & bottom left © Doug Perrine/Seapics.com, bottom right© Phillip Colla/Seapics.com, middle & bottom © Doug Perrine/Seapics.com; p.112 © Bob Cranston/Seapics.com; p.113 © Jeremy Stafford-Deitsch.Seapics.com; p.115 © Mako Hirose/Seapics.com; p.116 © Mark Strickland/Seapics.com; p.117 © Mako Hirose/Seapics.com; p.118 top © Marilyn Kazmers/Seapics.com, bottom © Doug Perrine/Seapics.com; p.120 © Tom Campbell; p.121 © Jurgen Freund/ Nature Picture Library; p.122 © Jeff Rotman/BBC Natural History Unit.

All other images are copyright of the Natural History Museum, London

ACKNOWLEDGEMENTS
I would like to thank Philip Vass, IUCN Shark Specialist Group, staff in the Department of Zoology at the Natural History Museum, London, and two anonymous reviewers from the USA for their valuable comments and suggestions on recent shark research worldwide. I would like also to thank our editor Jonathan Elphick for recovering meaningful fragments of the English language.